Cultural and Emotional Rootlessness

Cultural and Emotional Rootlessness

FOUR CENTRAL FOUNDATIONS FOR TRAUMA HEALING

ALFRED C. JARYAN JR., LMFT

ISBN 13: 978-1-63489-846-1
Library of Congress Catalog Number has been applied for.
Printed in the United States of America
First Printing: 2026
30 29 28 27 26 5 4 3 2 1

Cover design by Geronna Lewis-Lyte (geronna.com)
Interior design by Dan Pitts (danpitts.com)
Edited by Jacques Lesure and Kate Leibfried
Proofread by Abbie Phelps and Emma Kaiser
Production editing by Victoria Petelin

Wise Ink Media
PO Box 580195
Minneapolis, MN 55458-0195
wiseink.com

Wise Ink is a creative publishing agency for game-changers. Wise Ink authors uplift, inspire, and inform, and their titles support building a better and more equitable world. For more information, visit wiseink.com.

To order, visit itascabooks.com. Reseller discounts available.

DEDICATION

This book is dedicated to Jesus Christ, my Lord and Savior, who has blessed me with the knowledge, understanding, and wisdom to share the gift of healing with others worldwide. I am grateful for the opportunity to contribute to the journey of healing and growth.

The Lord is my shepherd; I shall not want.
—Psalm 23:1

Also, to all my friends, family members, and loved ones around the world, thank you for your support. May you also endure, overcome, and wholly thrive in life.

DISCLAIMER

The concepts and tools presented in this book, especially those discussing trauma, are not meant to replace consultations with a licensed mental health professional. The content of this book is for informational purposes only and is not intended to diagnose, treat, cure, or prevent any condition or disease. Please consult your physician or health care/mental health specialist regarding the suggestions and recommendations in this book. The publisher and author make no guarantees concerning the level of success you may experience by following the advice and strategies in this book.

TABLE OF CONTENTS

AUTHOR MESSAGE

I am a licensed marriage and family therapist who offers a method of healing the trauma from displacement with the Four C's: Curiosity, Compassion, Creativity, and Courage. Together, these four practices help to build authentic support networks. The rootless body needs healing to flow toward a wholly healed life. Other treatments may include medication through a professional medical doctor/prescriber, mental health or psychotherapy, yoga, trauma-focused EMDR therapeutic support, neurofeedback therapy, daily self- or other-guided meditation practices, self-reflections, daily questions found in this book, positive self-talk practices, and compassionate self-nurturing.

My thirty-five-year journey began in Monrovia, Liberia, in West Africa, before transitioning to the United States to live as an immigrant in Western society. Mine is a story of pain, suffering, and eventually finding peace after healing through living as my most authentic self—living with the whole truth in my immigrant body. Despite this being my story, trauma is a universal issue, and no one is immune to its damage. We all carry immigrant roots in unique ways, whether through family history (generational), personal history, or primary experiences from different homelands outside US or Western soil.

Because I found and recreated myself, my goal is to encourage others to do the same without fear-driven self-judgments. If you embody the confidence to trust whatever painful reality comes into your life and face these challenges with a calm and confident mind, soul, and body, you are on the right path to becoming whole and functioning in life. When we decide to heal consciously, pain holds a new meaning in our lives. It is now a gift to overcome, which we fully control. To feel authentic and whole again, I encourage embracing a curious open mind, a compassionate heart, creative nurturing, courageous beliefs, and caring, loving practices.

Acknowledgment of Land: Today, eleven tribal nations and communities are located within Minnesota, the place Wise Ink calls home. Wise Ink pays tribute to the Dakota and Ojibwe as the original people of this sacred land, first called Mni Sota Makoce in the Dakota language. Mni Sota Makoce is a place that carries a deep, layered history across the thousands of years the Dakota and Ojibwe peoples have been in kinship with the land and in the centuries since European settlers colonized the land that Minnesota now occupies. The land seizures and genocide committed by the United States were projects of spiritual and cultural destruction that denied the Dakota free and unhindered access to the land that fundamentally shaped their identity. We acknowledge that trauma has occurred, that harm continues to happen today, and that it is incumbent upon all of us residing on this land to work toward an equitable future where everyone can thrive. We encourage you, too, to learn and consider the history of the land you reside in and the resilient peoples and complex legacies that have made it what it is today.

CHAPTER 1

ALFRED'S JOURNEY

War changes the mind. It certainly changed mine. My early days in Liberia were full of stories that set the course for the challenges and journeys I would one day embark on. For context, imagine you are eight years old in 1997 (as I was), witnessing historic levels of unrest in Liberia during a civil war where looting was a normal occurrence and rebels would often go door-to-door and loot neighborhood homes during the night. They would break down front doors, taking clothing and rice back to their rebel camps. This was their normal method of gaining resources, and it often involved destruction and harm, with rebels holding people at gunpoint or beating them. This travesty happened to a neighbor across the street from our family's house. I watched the rebels loot our neighbors, hoping they wouldn't come to our home next. My heart was racing like never before, and I felt paralyzed.

A week later, it happened to us. The rebels came at night, and before we could prepare, they were banging on the door. They then used a hammer-like piece of black metal to penetrate our front door. The noise was deafening, and my family was screaming while they entered forcibly. During the break-in and looting at our house, my cousin was at my uncle's house with a different rebel group. Their house was located next door, facing our backyard, and my cousin heard the commotion. The rebel group took a position at the back of our house while the looters and opposing rebel groups were divided inside the house, with some standing guard in our front yard. My cousin and his rebel group were in the right place at the right time on that terrifying night. Both groups had their weapons ready to shoot while engaging in intense communication.

My cousin told the opposing rebel group to leave and not hurt anyone; otherwise, everyone would die. My cousin's rebel group covered the back of the house, trying to secure the rooms where we slept. But that's where several rebels were holding my family at gunpoint in the dark. We all huddled together in one room—my mother, my father, my siblings, our extended family members, and me.

One rebel had his AK-47 rifle pointed at my father, and another had his gun aimed at my mother and me. Sitting on my mother's lap on the bed, I stared at the gun. The rebels were yelling at us, "Don't move!" My father stood next to the bed, facing the open room. A rebel held a gun to his head, shouting, "Where's your car key and rice bags?" Food was scarce during wartime. Rebels regularly broke into civilian houses to take food, along with any material things of value they could utilize. My father kept saying, as calmly as possible, "I do not know where the car key is." But the rebel kept yelling, "Tell me where the key is or I'll blow your head off!" The car in question was my father's gold midsize SUV, which was parked in our garage.

The intensity of loud, screaming voices continued until my cousin and his group of rebels intervened and drew weapons against the other rebel group. Facing the dreadful situation, I was filled with terror, but my mother held me tightly. Feeling powerless, I tried to come to terms with what might happen. Looking at the gun, I wondered when it would be fired and how much it would hurt. I hoped for a quick end.

After a while, my cousin told the opposing rebel group that his group would allow them to walk away without any gunfire, as long as they did not hurt anyone. This led to a ceasefire, with the leader of the looting rebels agreeing to the deal and telling his men to stand down and leave. In the moment, I felt relieved, but for the rest of the night and all that week, I was numb with shock. It was hard to believe that my life came so close to danger at such a young age, even though looting and rebel break-ins were common during the war. Today, I am still working on healing from the fear and trauma caused by that situation.

After our house was broken into in Liberia, we lived in constant fear of rebel attacks. This fear consumed our lives. Every time the sun went down and the looting started, a part of me hoped my cousin and his rebel group would return to protect us, but we never saw them again. Though we did not experience another break-in, the sounds of war made a constant background soundtrack of chaos and confusion in the streets of Paynesville, Liberia, a suburb of Monrovia located in Montserrado County, which was populated by about half a million people. It was normal for me to lie on the floor of my family home to feel more protected from errant bullets or shells, hoping they wouldn't pierce my innocent skin.

From that point on, I knew my most important lessons in life would not be taught in the schoolhouse. Instead, I would be taught through the trials, tribulations, and lived experiences of the fifteen people who were living in my house. My parents, siblings, and extended family were crammed in a three-bedroom house without electricity and running water during one of the most atrocious civil wars to date, the First Liberian Civil War, which lasted from 1989 to 1997. Stability was only a dream, so we kept packs of clothing and food in case we needed to vacate to safety. My father realized it was becoming too dangerous to stay in Liberia, so he decided to leave for the United States ahead of the rest of the family. My uncle was already there, and my father hoped to set up a stable situation before sending for us.

My father's absence made me more afraid to lose my mother, sister, brother, grandmother, aunts, uncles, and cousins to violence. I felt terrified (at times visibly shaking), certain of our impending doom. I was scared for my life and the lives of my family members, and I could not see a way for us to survive. It felt like being trapped in darkness with no way out. Fear overwhelmed me, and I worried excessively every minute, hour, and day, never knowing if the next round of gunshots would be the one to end our lives. Uncertainty and constant fear were our companions. I was afraid my father would never send for us, and we would never see him again. I worried that the war would tear our family apart and constantly feared that, one day, my family would be gone forever.

My mother played the role of supporter, rallying my spirits as I tried to make sense of the senselessness, one dark day at a time. Throughout my childhood, my mother lovingly cared for me in countless ways. She dedicatedly prepared nourishing meals, like rice and beef soup, ensuring I had at least two wholesome meals daily. In addition to providing for my basic needs, she also delighted in buying me new clothes and toys, even surprising me with a soccer ball once, and she encouraged me to stay active and playful. Not only did she tend to my physical needs, but she also played an active role in my education. She maintained regular communication with my teachers to ensure I was thriving in school, showing an unwavering commitment to my academic success. Beyond all this, she also ensured I was spiritually supported. Every Sunday morning, my mother woke me up early, prepared breakfast, and helped me get ready for church. Together, we walked to the church, attending Sunday worship services and praising Jesus Christ. This weekly tradition was a powerful reminder of the values she held dear, and it instilled in me a deep sense of faith and community. These were the realities of my early days, which played a huge role in how I understand myself today.

My family's primary focus was to survive in our perilous environment. I grew accustomed to life's pains, but was always fearful of the unknown. Dealing with the hardships of such a challenging reality was harsh, mainly because of the trauma I experienced during the civil war, which I endured until my family moved when I was ten years old. Letting our guard down could have been fatal in such a hostile environment.

During this time, I leaned on two main tenets: courage and faith. Embodying these principles during tough times can help us persevere and believe in ourselves during the storm and after it calms. Hebrews 1:1 defines faith as the assurance of things hoped for, the conviction of things not seen. As you rebuild your life, have faith in your dreams—your conviction will give you the drive to live them. My faith only amplified after our home invasion, since the presence of my cousin and his rebel group at my uncle's house felt like a miracle. Our survival that day was only possible through the grace of my Lord and Savior, Jesus Christ. Surviving this experience showed me that, as long as you are alive, there is reason to hope.

However, trapped in circumstances defined by fear and trauma, it took me a long time to appreciate the strength these experiences gave me. Fear dominated my life in Liberia and followed me to the United States.

From Refugee to Therapist

I was born in the John F. Kennedy Memorial Hospital, a national medical center located in the Sinkor district of Monrovia, Liberia, on May 20, 1989, to my parents, Alfred and Mary Jaryan. They named me after my father: Alfred C. Jaryan Jr. Due to food insecurity, I was born malnourished and my growth was stunted; I was underweight, lacked essential nutrients, and had a weak immune system, all of which can hurt a person's ability to see, taste, and smell, in addition to increasing the risk for anxiety and mood disorders. After my birth, the doctors gave little hope for my survival, warning my mother to prepare for the worst. However, I defeated the odds and began to recover, gain weight, and surprise everyone with my progress. Eventually, I left the hospital and started a new life with my loving family.

Life is a series of transformations and rebirths. For those who have faced multiple life-threatening situations, any big life change can bring your worst memories to the surface. Fear contaminates every experience, even the positive ones.

Survival instincts pressure refugees to take life-threatening risks to escape. Their survival minds tell them they may not live long or that they will suffer if they stay in their homeland. People escaping their homeland continue to run from their nightmares long after immigrating to a new country. In my family's case, we were confused, hopeless, and powerless in the dark space of our homeland. I became an expert survivalist, prepped to die in a fight or escape my childhood home on foot if gunshots sounded nearby. After what I had seen and experienced, how could I ever feel safe? After growing up in Paynesville, Liberia, I had no idea what to expect when my father finally told us it was time to come to the United States. I was skeptical and afraid.

Through a lottery immigration process known as the diversity visa program, my family left for the United States in 1999 to escape the war. My mother, sister, eldest brother, and I arrived at Roberts International Airport in Liberia, where we said goodbye to our extended family and boarded a plane. Our first stop was the Ivory Coast, a bordering country to the west of Liberia, where we spent an approximately three-hour layover at the Félix-Houphouët-Boigny International Airport in Abidjan, resting and waiting for our flight to the United States. After the layover, we boarded the plane and took off.

The thirteen-hour flight landed us at John F. Kennedy International Airport in Queens, New York, where my uncle picked us up and drove us to his high-rise apartment in Trenton, New Jersey. We lived in Trenton for our first month in the United States, slowly getting used to life in the US and enjoying American fast food, like burgers and KFC. After spending one month in Trenton, we packed our belongings, said our goodbyes, and embarked on a fourteen-hour drive in my uncle's car to Iowa City, Iowa, where we met my father. There, we spent our first two years on US soil. Meanwhile, a second civil war broke out in Liberia. My extended family was trapped in the conflict an ocean away, while I was in a strange new place, unable to help them or know if they would be all right.

Later in life, long after the Second Liberian Civil War had concluded, I decided to pursue graduate studies to better understand my experiences and those of the many others who had experienced cultural rootlessness and displacement. Along the journey, I realized that to build a sense of cultural "rootedness," a person must first become comfortable in their identity through a positive relationship with themselves. Support from others, while important, cannot replace the stability and peace that come from self-acceptance, self-compassion, and self-trust. Community support is not a fix-all for one's issues, nor can we expect it to be. In my case, it was critical for me to find safety in my own mind and body while assimilating into US society. This journey wasn't easy, and I shied away from reality for a long time through unhealthy, unconscious avoidance tactics like addiction to alcohol, impulsive actions, and self-condemnation. However, as I grew up and became a therapist, I developed four crucial inner resources that helped me regain confidence, eschew my destructive habits, and move forward. Those resources, which I call the **Four Central Healing Foundations**, are an antidote to the loneliness, displacement, and loss of identity that often accompany the refugee experience.

It is undeniable that my experience during the war informed my style as a counselor and therapist, making me especially compassionate and empathetic. Additionally, my ability to continually engage in self-therapeutic work, which I call "healing," is central to my life and aids my work. By constantly giving myself the power to choose how to nurture, care, and love myself daily, I can be more authentic in my sessions with clients. I pay attention to my emotions and body language, reducing the urge to project my pain onto the clients I am helping. I disclose my experiences when I believe they could benefit the client's healing journey, but I am in control of when and how I share these experiences—they no longer govern my emotions or haunt my daily life as they once did.

In trauma, we lose our power of choice. To free ourselves from a life ruled by trauma, it is essential to nurture ourselves and allow ourselves, and others, the freedom to choose our paths and make everyday decisions. With choice in mind, it is essential to be honest with ourselves and our loved ones. For example, before sharing my trauma-filled background, I explain my intentions to the client and give them the power to choose whether they want to hear how my experiences have influenced my practice as a therapist. I aim to let my clients see me beyond my professional title and view me as a human being on a collaborative healing journey with them.

Another factor that helped mold me into a compassionate therapist is my mother's unconditional love. She remained steadfast and supportive through our shared traumatic experiences, which has helped me, in turn, meet my clients where they are in their healing journeys. I consciously use active listening skills, model positive communication behaviors, and empower clients by asking how to support them best. Through this approach, I help them reframe their perspectives on pain, emphasizing that hurting is a normal part of life and does not have to hinder their abilities to love themselves again. I also employ reflection questions, asking clients about their experiences of nurturing, care, and love from their parents or caregivers before encouraging them to think about how they want to nurture, care for, and love themselves.

My childhood experiences with my mother underscore the importance of using a strength- and solution-oriented nurturing approach as a therapist, regardless of pain or cultural background. Providing authentic verbal support can lead to genuine changes in thinking and behavior. Regardless of upbringing, as adults, we can learn to support ourselves and develop better, more authentic lives. It is essential to explore our own minds, reactions, impulses, and beliefs to heal our pain. We cannot shame or force our way out of pain, but we must instead offer ourselves love, patience, and choices, which create a stable foundation for us to return to as we courageously pursue the lives we want. Whether we received the nurturing we needed as children or not, we must continue evolving our self-nurturing, caring, and loving patterns as adults, especially in the face of unhealed traumas and new challenges.

The start of my life was painful, dark, and ugly. To alter one's life, an individual must flow and expand in tandem with their current life, not live in patterns of the past. People who have experienced devastating trauma in childhood often experience a multitude of difficulties, including finding meaning in their present lives. Immigrants who have lived in a war-ravaged, impoverished nation often enter the United States psychologically traumatized, carrying the tangible and intangible marks of a gravely damaged psyche, heart, spirit, and body. This damage can lead to unhealthy reflections, decreased feelings of self-worth, difficulty in calming raging emotions, depression, and more. Additionally, trauma survivors often engage in activities that could result in painful consequences because of unresolved wounds. These factors—trauma, psychological and physical damage, and unhealthy activities or outlets—can perpetuate falsehoods and trap people in their earlier traumas, keeping them from healing and demanding healthier living standards in their community.

While building my therapy practice and attempting to heal from past trauma, I developed the four authentic central healing foundations. These foundations helped me build my dreams fully in the United States. This book is the result of my therapy work (applied both to myself and to my clients) and developed from my curiosity about healing. My passion is to give these four resources to others who are trapped inside their unhealed traumatic experiences.

I am a Liberian American, a survivor of civil war, a licensed therapist, and a community healer for those who feel rootless. It is my goal that all immigrants can one day heal from what I call cultural rootlessness—the specific trauma that comes from being forced to leave your home and settle in a new culture—a phenomenon that is far-reaching, painful, and life-changing. I have chosen to share my story with you to vulnerably show how my immigration experience impacted my identity, and to remind immigrants everywhere that they, too, can take control of their healing. I am proud to have lived through an abrupt relocation to an entirely new culture, and I am proud of you for choosing to go on this healing journey with me.

CHAPTER 2

CULTURAL ROOTLESSNESS AND POSSIBLE SOLUTIONS

Despite the pain you've experienced, it is within your power to create a joyful life. When I feel completely hopeless, I remind myself of those moments in my life that held the most beauty, safety, and meaning. You must remember that positive experiences are possible and they will come to you again. Although human beings are very good at remembering the negative aspects of our circumstances, we often mistake these things for the total truth. In reality, our struggles are multifaceted and complex. Despite the war, I had a range of support and grounding moments in which I was held gently, spoken to softly, or even shared a full-belly laugh with my family and friends. While these moments could never erase the pain and harm I experienced, they certainly make my memories and recollection of events more complex.

I am reminded of my time eating the sweet fruit from the mango tree in front of our yard, playing in the sandbox with my younger cousins, and upholding my family's Lorma traditions—the traditions of our tribe. We spoke our tribal language, in addition to Liberian-English. Growing up, Lorma tribal tunes flowed through my body, captivating me with their fast style and energetic drum patterns. Other everyday joys included sitting in my dad's lap while the breeze skated past us, entertaining ourselves with toys, or gambling for marbles in our shared yards (a skill that

I worked hard to master). We'd play soccer in the yard with makeshift goalposts until our feet hurt from kicking the ball around. Sometimes the games ballooned into six-on-six matches against other neighborhoods.

As kids, we didn't shy away from a little mischief and would sometimes take mangoes from our neighbors' yards, even though we had our own. Our parents made us apologize and do work for them to reconcile for our wrongdoing. We loved stealing the mangoes because our neighbors had different varieties than we did, so the extra labor was well worth it. Other treats were store-bought. I remember walking to the market with a couple dollars for cookies or candies, or patronizing the milk-candy truck that would pass through our neighborhood at the same time each day. I also remember my gracious uncle giving me money for snacks.

Despite the atrocities, I was basking in the cultural practices and everyday life of my homeland. I was experiencing political upheaval and instability, but ultimately, I was rooted in my family, my neighborhood, and the rhythm of my daily life.

Of course, I will always remember the devastation of the war and, as a therapist, I immediately notice the mindset of the immigrants who have experienced similar circumstances. In my experience, many refugees deal with their trauma internally and carry a prevailing notion that "the war continues." They seem to struggle to move beyond surviving to thriving in life. My mom used to say that the war would never finish, that she was hopeless for the state of Liberia, and that the origins of our struggles said a lot about who we were. While this might come off as pessimistic to many, I see this viewpoint as informed by her own experiences. I am reminded of a conversation with my mother in which she emphasized that I am a survivor. I understood her to mean that my challenges have built resilience and endurance within me, preparing me to overcome difficult life situations.

My mother's struggles have made her compassionate and empathetic. In turn, she encouraged me to actively listen to others without judgment and accept people for who they are without attempting to change them to fit my expectations. I've noticed that younger refugees are using humor as a coping mechanism to deflect from the pain and hardships endured during war. This has led to a persistent avoidance of addressing and dealing with deep-rooted trauma. Effective communication is lacking, hindering the healing process from war-related trauma. The difference in experiences between the older and younger generations has led to a lack of understanding between them. For example, the older generation experienced Liberia before the civil war in the 1990s, while the younger generation mostly remembers the country during the war. Many younger Liberians struggle to relate to the idea of a peaceful and prosperous Liberia, as their experiences are predominantly associated with violence, looting, and other traumatic events. Their sorrow, expressed through humor, is often cynical and apathetic. It is not the same as the sorrow of older generations.

However, there is a thread of hope represented in this narrative, despite the circumstances. The situation is gradually changing within the Liberian community due to the support and resources provided to younger and older generations. Access to mental health support, medical aid, and essential resources in both the United States and Liberia is helping to alleviate some of the trauma.

I share this background information about Liberia and my personal experiences to help empower you to explore how your past experiences have shaped your present perceptions of self and the life you are choosing to live daily. It is important to become aware of the link between the past and present, including how you currently function in society. This awareness can help make the nurturing, caring, and loving changes we all desire in life.

I also hope to convey that healing is always possible through hope and the unconditional support of others and ourselves. Hope plays a crucial role in overcoming challenges and facilitating healing. It enables us to look past our wounds and envision a better reality, and it empowers us to strive for positive change. On the other hand, hopelessness traps us in our pain and suffering, diminishing our desire to support ourselves and others consistently. Therefore, we must actively choose hope over despair and encourage others to do the same. We can better equip ourselves to seek and utilize supportive community resources by embracing hope instead of despair.

The practice of hopefulness stands in opposition to hopelessness by helping us detach from despair linked to past traumas. It anchors us in the present while encouraging us to look toward the future with trust and a healing perspective. When healing from cultural rootlessness, it is essential to recognize that hopefulness is a powerful antidote to the despair that often arises from unhealed experiences. This hope is not merely a fleeting emotion; it is an active force based on our daily belief in our ability to overcome past and present challenges, illuminating our path forward with genuine confidence.

By embracing hope, we cultivate a reflective and forward-thinking mindset, which allows us to envision a future filled with blessings and healing opportunities. Adopting this hopeful perspective helps us navigate our journey with trust and resilience, enabling us to build or strengthen authentic cultural identities and foster meaningful relationships grounded in understanding, support, healing, and a deeper appreciation for life.

Despite the trauma my homeland has endured, I know that Liberians are currently receiving support on their healing journeys, with many resources available to enable their paths toward recovery. This demonstrates how healing is possible for individuals, families, and cultural groups affected by rootlessness traumas, especially when they receive ongoing care, nurturance, and loving resources to address the long-term consequences of their suffering.

When we were attempting to escape civil war, my family relied heavily on external resources, including the crucial "diversity visa" granted to us through a United States asylum program. This visa afforded my mother, father, sister, eldest brother, and I the chance to pursue our aspirations in the US. It was a blessing but also a matter of faith. The immigration process is long and arduous. Even after the US government agrees to grant asylum, immigrants must coordinate with someone who will commit to sponsor them and jump over many other hurdles, many of which involve extensive paperwork. Since there was no internet access when we emigrated, my parents would take extra precautions to keep our documents safe, hiding them in the attic in a spot only they knew.

It was hard to discuss the emmigration process with family because everybody wanted to leave, but only a limited number of people could legally emigrate. We kept our acceptance into the US quiet until it was nearly time to depart. We had to protect our privacy, but it was very tough to keep information from the rest of our family. When I learned my dad was heading to the Midwestern US, I didn't even know where the United States was located. Our future sponsors lived in Iowa and were key to helping my family emigrate. While we kept our upcoming trip from our extended family in Liberia, we were placing a lot of trust in our sponsor family in Iowa. We didn't know them beforehand, and we wondered if they would be able to fully understand the situation we were coming from.

The Western world has always struggled to comprehend (or has purposefully ignored) the political upheaval in postcolonial Africa. It's rarely discussed due to white-centered mainstream media, popular debates, and other forums of discussion for social and political problems. My family is a case study for the gravity of the conflicts that have occurred and continue to take place, and it is important for Westerners to think through their connections to immigrant and refugee experiences and consider the context. Whose narratives and stories are predominant and widely known? How do we perceive the challenges of others based on our own social location and identities? The war that tore apart my family and devastated my home country barely registered in the white-centric culture of the US, which tends to think about Africa as a whole, not bothering to learn about the different cultures, conflicts, and countries within it. It was a challenge to realize that most people I interacted with didn't have the context to understand what I'd been through or where I'd come from. Though people were friendly, I felt rootless and isolated in a new country where few people understood or talked about the Liberian civil war that had changed my entire life. Through my work as a therapist, and by talking with other refugees, I have learned that my experience is hardly unique. Many refugees feel a gap between their adopted home and themselves, brought about by the indifference or ignorance of others, and the nation's tendency to gloss over conflicts and other significant events in countries where the population is primarily not white. They feel separated by oceans of cultural differences and a lack of understanding.

As a child, I only understood the war in broad terms. This period of angst and turmoil, while terrifying, was my normal. However, I now know that the civil war in Liberia had roots in cultural trauma that existed long before I was born. Between 1820 and 1843, 4,571 free and recently emancipated African Americans left the US to found the country of Liberia, though only 1,819 survived the trip and integrated with the tribal indigenous groups in the region. Their arrival started years of tension between the tribal groups and those descended from enslaved African Americans, known as Americo-Liberians, who came to the region to start new lives. The Americo-Liberians held political power in Liberia until the 1980s, when members of indigenous tribes began to support Samuel Doe, who became the first Liberian president of tribal descent.

Doe's militant and punitive leadership split the movement for more tribal representation in government into competing groups. Doe favored his own tribe, the Krahn, while other indigenous tribes felt betrayed by his lack of support. The First Liberian Civil War, lasting between 1989 and 1997, claimed the lives of two hundred thousand Liberians, driving many civilians to other countries. Doe's main opponent, Charles Taylor, founded the National Patriotic Front of Liberia, which led a series of attacks that left Monrovia in flames and hundreds of thousands of people fleeing. Taylor's own movement split off into another group called the Independent National Patriotic Front of Liberia. Doe's supporters, Taylor's supporters, and the INPFL were all fighting for power.

The Second Liberian Civil War started in 1999, a continuation of the instability and resentment from the first civil war. By this point, I was ten years old and had endured a significant period of political upheaval. When I left for the US, the war raged on until a ceasefire agreement was reached in 2003. The Liberian Truth and Reconciliation Commission stated that over 250,000 people had died, leaving an unstable economy and one million Liberians displaced from their homes. The wars caused significant issues with Liberia's health care system, education, workforce, and almost every other area of social and economic life. The impacts of those wars still affect the over five million people living in Liberia today.

Liberian troops involved children as young as nine years old in the war, both boys and girls. By their standards, nobody was too young to hold a gun and kill during the First Liberian Civil War. Children in Liberia were enlisted as soldiers because they followed the instructions of their superiors on the battlefield. As a result of this exploitation, Liberia and its citizens would go on to experience generations of restlessness and chaos. I first learned about the existence of child soldiers after I moved to the United States and learned about the second civil war that took place in Liberia. It was a shocking revelation, as I had never encountered such a concept while living in Liberia. The stories I heard from my parents, family members, and others in the United States, as well as my own experiences during the first civil war, shed light on the fact that my own experiences were only the tip of the iceberg.

Cultural Rootlessness Through Vicarious and Secondary Trauma

It wasn't until much later in my life that I realized I was experiencing cultural rootlessness trauma through vicarious and secondary trauma. Secondary and vicarious trauma are both mental health conditions that evolve from another person's traumatic experiences. *Vicarious trauma* is a term coined in the 1990s by Irene Lisa McCann and Laurie Anne Pearlman. This type of trauma develops over time through repeat exposure to someone else's traumatic experiences. Symptoms of vicarious trauma may include ongoing fears, a shift in worldview, and feelings of hopelessness, fatigue, and overwhelm. Vicarious trauma can alter one's worldview and even change one's sense of self through empathic bonding, exposure to graphic traumatizing experiences, exposure to cruelty, and reenactment of the trauma.

Around the same time, the phenomenon known as secondary trauma was coined in 1995 by Charles Figley. Secondary traumatic stress typically occurs suddenly after a single exposure to trauma, such as hearing someone else's traumatic story, and leads to symptoms of intrusive thoughts, avoidance, and hyperarousal in society.

Refugees and children of refugees often experience vicarious and secondary trauma. While I did not live in Liberia during the second civil war, I heard of the violence and its consequences through my family and other Liberians in the US. Hearing about the violence made me more afraid of the world. As a young person, I avoided any people, places, things, or situations that reminded me of my past Liberian war experiences. I witnessed and heard their pain, their cries for help, and their struggles.

The Black Immigrant Experience in the United States

US culture places a big emphasis on the freedom to pursue one's dreams, especially when people talk about the immigrant experience. Before I could do this, however, I had to conquer being uprooted from my culture, develop empathy for myself, learn to diminish my anxiety, surmount vicarious trauma, and work toward healing. I had to overcome some of my haunting memories, the persistence of worry, and the fear that paralyzed me. I learned to do this within the context of the United States, which came with many of its own challenges. Regardless, I was committed to doing it. I understood that my inner voice was a projection of my ancestors and my spiritual higher power (God) helping me discover myself.

My ancestors called me to understand my cultural story beyond my individual experience, absorbing it through a broader group perspective. Instead of focusing solely on what happened to me, I asked myself: What happened to *us*, my Liberian people? What has happened to all immigrants and refugees who endure wars and trauma? How did we become culturally rootless in the United States, and how can we overcome it? Through my journey, I realized that connecting with my higher spiritual power plays a significant role in healing rootlessness, as these nurturing forces continually empower me to pray, meditate, think openly, love compassionately, live courageously by faith, and trust my creative expression of self to flow without judgments each day of my life.

To heal, it is crucial to be aware of our past experiences independently and interdependently. Understanding the experiences of the generations that preceded us helps us recognize the depth of our struggles. Exploring my ancestors' journeys has taught me that the root of my struggle did not begin with my life; trauma was also a reality for them. This understanding has helped me explore how such traumatic experiences have been passed down through different Liberian generations, affecting individuals, families, and social functioning. To heal more fully, we must delve into the entirety of our stories and our backgrounds. We cannot truly heal without understanding the full scope of our experiences.

This realization is the main reason I pursued a career as a mental health professional. I wanted to help other marginalized people, such as immigrants to the United States, work through their experiences and become healthier people.

We often homogenize the experiences of all immigrants based on one idea of "US culture." However, there is no singular US culture into which one can integrate. Your immigration experience is as unique as a snowflake, and it is formed by where you came from, where you settled in the US, how that place shifts, and the people surrounding you. These social, political, and cultural influences are important to consider. I have lived throughout the Midwest, often in places where Black immigrants were rare. Wherever I went, I made an effort to discuss my specific experiences (if others were open to it), hoping that others would feel empowered to also share their unique stories.

Despite our unique circumstances, immigrants and refugees often have some overlapping experiences that are useful to consider, regardless of race, ethnicity, class, gender, sexuality, physical ability, mental capacity or other forms of identity. However, context also matters in terms of how we capture immigrant experiences. Many advocacy organizations have started to use **a multi-diverse healing approach** to understand the needs of specific populations. In this context, "multi-diverse" means utilizing more than one resource at a time for support. This can include a combination of psychotherapy, medication, spiritual healing, culturally specific healing practices, individual therapy, group therapy, family therapy, and art or music therapy. Addressing healing across multiple dimensions and contexts is essential to effectively support each person's needs. This approach also provides healers with resources that continually empower them to grow authentically in their own lives.

A multi-diverse approach acknowledges that we are complex humans who may need to approach healing from many different angles. This allows us to put a magnifying glass on the interwoven and interconnected ways that multiple identities create a unique story. This approach also allows us to better express and communicate our authentic stories.

While the data is lacking due to the ways in which racial demographics in immigration data are captured, a recent Immigration Impact report estimates that the Black immigrant population increased by 23.5 percent over the past decade. In 2012, there were approximately 3.5 million Black immigrants, and by 2022 that number increased to 4.3 million (American Immigration Council Staff, 2024). Another source, the Black Alliance for Just Immigration, claims that millions of Black residents are noncitizens, a category that has grown exponentially since the time my family came to the United States. It is apparent that as time goes on, a larger number of Black Americans will be foreign-born, constituting a new burgeoning community that will carry its own challenges, traumas, and strengths. This is important to note because, within these small but growing numbers, we can better imagine the weight of transition that so many people are facing.

The Black immigrant community is a complex and dynamic group that requires attention. Often, the experiences of Black immigrants are pushed aside as non-normative or not large enough in scale to inform policy solutions or even counseling approaches. However, these numbers reveal that those notions are misaligned with the data.

In addition to the number of Black immigrants arriving to the US, the Black Alliance for Just Immigration also reports on the diversity of countries of origin. For example, it is estimated that the majority of foreign-born Black people in the United States were born in Jamaica and Haiti. In terms of the continent of Africa, most immigrants to the United States are from Nigeria and Ethiopia. There are various timelines in which Black immigrants are likely to have resided in the US, depending on country of origin. For example, Black Caribbeans had a history of immigrating to the US as early as the 1960s. This information is important to know, since some groups of Black immigrants may be experiencing more rootlessness, or more integration, than others.

It is without question that immigrants and refugees endure formidable difficulties that deserve attention, reflection, and proper consideration. Every individual's story of displacement is unique. Tales of cultural unrooting could include civil war, being uprooted from one's home due to violence or natural disaster, or becoming separated from family members or cherished ones.

Author Bessel van der Kolk, MD, claims in *The Body Keeps the Score*, "The consequences of traumatic experiences can be seen in the realms of our psyche and emotions, our capability to be happy and connected, and even our biology and immunity." Trauma affects not only those who experience it, but also those in their vicinity. Immigrants living in the United States are continually concerned about the risks their relatives in their native land are subjected to, including violence, destitution, the possibility of famine, maltreatment, lack of shelter, and political conflict. The consequences of these current traumas linger and shape our reactions to everyday life. We must invest in our capacity to heal from past traumas so they no longer interfere with present experiences. Our traumas affect our ideas, convictions, sentiments, and perceptions of ourselves and our current circumstances.

In the world, we live our best lives from the inside out, meaning that we trust our inner voices to lead our bodies toward full health after trauma. When we focus on living from the inside out, it is easy to see and value the power of choice in healing and the power of knowing your past self. If you want to create a more authentic present and future, you must return to the source of your unhealed traumatic damage, wounds, and pain. For many Black immigrants, that could involve the sometimes painful work of deep reflection, talking over traumatic events with others, turning to a qualified therapist, or forgiving ourselves or others for wrongdoings. It may also involve finding a community of supportive people who share a common background and can collaborate to uplift each other.

Part of this healing journey will inevitably involve reflection and self-awareness. Many past and present philosophers have talked about the importance of self-awareness and self-trust—teachers such as Socrates (the father of self-control ideology), Marcus Aurelius (stoic philosopher), and Eckhart Tolle (renowned spiritual teacher and author). It is necessary to promote healing both internally and externally to live a full life. We can rely on our own inner mental capabilities to help us fight against external influences. When we are young, we cannot take care of ourselves and must rely on the external world to provide for us. If that external world is dangerous and unpredictable (as is the case for many immigrants from the African continent), we may never form the necessary inner foundations to ever feel safe. The same thing can happen after someone experiences trauma. If we become "unrooted," we are unable to trust or connect to life, the people around us, or ourselves. In undergoing healing work as adults, we must develop a sense of "rootedness" not to the external environment or home, but to ourselves. This means finding safety and comfort in who we are, in what we value, and in our abilities.

Traumatic events that have caused us harm continue to influence us long after the physical effects of that trauma have ended. It is my hope to enable you to live in freedom without the burden of guilt, shame, and continuous suffering, while being able to support yourself and survive. Becoming proficient in the art of genuine self-exploration supports a harmonious combination of mind, body, and environment. Through dreaming and taking intentional steps in your healing journey, you can create a new reality as a Black immigrant in the United States.

Exploring Cultural Rootlessness

Cultural rootlessness describes the separation of the human being from their cultural foundations or identities. Culture shows us who we are and where we are headed in life. Roots represent where we come from in the world. Roots are also tied to our self-image, our values, and how well we can predict the world around us. Rootlessness starts with initial traumatic damage and continues with a person's failure to overcome trauma. Cultural rootlessness forces a person to adapt and survive with others in an unfamiliar society. It is the embodied form of many forms of harm—social isolation, discrimination, lack of resources—that one may encounter when navigating immigration. When the cultural body loses connection to its roots or foundations, immigrants and refugees stop knowing their authentic growing selves. They may keep surviving by embracing false personas, which causes pain and suffering until healing occurs within their inner and external worlds.

To comprehend the concept of cultural rootlessness trauma more profoundly, take a moment to reflect on a specific traumatic event that has significantly influenced your life. Consider how the echoes of that experience continue to shape your thoughts, emotions, and interactions long after the physical experience of the original event has passed. The persistent impact of such trauma serves as a potent reminder that it is not merely a fleeting moment, but rather an enduring source of familiar and different challenges that can manifest in various aspects of life.

Although immigrants have diverse experiences, certain emotional and behavioral patterns tend to emerge, many of which are linked to cultural rootlessness. A 2023 study by the Kaiser Family Foundation (KFF) and the *Los Angeles Times* illustrates some of the commonalities of the immigrant experience and the ways immigrants can feel disconnected from both their country of origin and their adopted home. Working with a sample size of 3,358 immigrant adults, the study is "the largest and most representative survey of immigrants living in the U.S. to date" (Schumacher et al., 2023).

One of the study's findings that relates to cultural rootlessness has to do with language. When living in one's home country, language is not typically much of a barrier. People communicate effortlessly, sharing the same formal language, slang, jokes, and idioms. When moving to a new country with a different primary language, that built-in comfort goes away. Even when an immigrant's grasp of the new language is decent, they may miss subtle cues that a native speaker would easily pick up on. This may cause frustration or feelings of isolation. The KFF/*LA Times* study found that over a third of immigrants were disparaged for speaking a language besides English, while 33 percent were told to "go back to where you came from." Poor treatment due to language differences affects immigrants in all parts of their lives, whether eating in a restaurant, visiting a clinic, interacting with law enforcement, or simply going to work.

Working in the United States is a challenge in itself. The KFF/*LA Times* study says, "Immigrants who are Black or Hispanic report disproportionate levels of discrimination at work, in their communities, and in health care settings." The majority of Black immigrants have dealt with workplace discrimination, and most (53 percent) are overqualified for their jobs. This group has had to navigate unfair or preferential treatment, harsh criticism, and microaggressions that their white peers do not typically face. For many people, work is closely tied to their identity and sense of self. If, like many immigrants, you feel out of place or uncomfortable in the workplace, that can lead to a sense of cultural rootlessness. You might feel unsupported or sense that you cannot talk with your peers in a meaningful way, due to the vast differences between you.

Another study I examined (Cabacungan, 2022) explored the personal processes that two immigrants went through as they co-created and negotiated their immigrant identities. This deep dive into the experiences of two immigrants from very different backgrounds—one Filipina, the other Iranian—illuminates how, even when hailing from different parts of the world, US immigrants share some common ground related to cultural rootlessness.

The study asked the participants questions about major life and historical events and the meaning they associated with them. The study found four overlapping themes across both the interviews. First, the participants spoke of similar reasons that prompted them to move to the United States, both mentioning financial hardship and community violence. Most families do not migrate for recreation—circumstances pressure them to uproot their whole lives and start anew. While there is some degree of choice in this, a refugee's agency and autonomy can feel limited when trying to survive.

Secondly, the participants spoke of the onset of anxiety, as well as the difficult but necessary adjustment they experienced upon arriving in the United States. Different language and politics created unique hurdles that aligned with larger dynamics in society.

Thirdly, both participants in this study used their professions to cope with their experiences. Between the medical field and literary studies, they both found outlets for their evolving selves to emerge. This is not dissimilar to my own journey of becoming a therapist.

Lastly, both participants said they felt a sense of inner conflict with a closeness to multiple identities. They suggested that identification as an American can be worn differently and cause greater belonging or conflict, depending on the context. For example, Cabacungan writes about how the Filipina participant felt like she could sometimes hold her Filipina identity within US society. However, the Persian man felt he needed to let go of his Persian identity due to factors such as the anti-immigrant sentiment. Regardless, both participants seemed to hold onto parts of their cultural heritage and identity to avoid what I call cultural rootlessness.

The Trauma Cycle

In addition to cultural rootlessness, many immigrants grapple with the emotional baggage and trauma that they've carried over from their past lives. Trauma starts as a painful, overwhelming experience that alters our worldview and the view of ourselves. If we experience trauma without processing it, that trauma tends to reappear in our lives as a cycle of negative behavior. In the trauma cycle, unhealed people develop the need to defend and protect against perceived dangers in society. The trauma cycle disrupts our ability to differentiate between hazards, threats, and safety.

The trauma cycle begins with a minimal, moderate, or detrimental life experience, such as enduring civil war; physical, emotional, or sexual abuse; neglect from parents or caregivers, abandonment; intimate partner violence; a difficult divorce or family breakup, displacement from one's childhood home or country; or any form of assault. The trauma cycle can also start with experiencing secondary or vicarious trauma, which involves witnessing, hearing, or reading about a traumatic experience that profoundly resonates with one's own life, such as witnessing family, loved ones, or close friends go through any of the aforementioned traumatic situations, or facing medical trauma with one's child. For instance, supporting a child diagnosed with cancer and undergoing chemotherapy can be incredibly traumatizing. These experiences do not just impact the individual going through the trauma but also affect their loved ones.

When our family and loved ones suffer, we grieve their pain deeply due to our emotional connections with them. Following personal, secondary, or vicarious traumatic experiences, individuals typically start to struggle internally. They find it challenging to soothe their recurring intrusive thoughts and ongoing fears about future scenarios related to their original traumas. This can lead to hypervigilance, self-doubt, negative thinking patterns and behaviors, and detachment from reality. It causes individuals to stop believing in themselves and begin to listen to their internal pain, with a lack of understanding about how to stop the recurring negative thinking patterns. As a result, they may behave in ways that reflect their self-doubt: a lack of confidence, increased isolation, angry outbursts, neglect of self-care, and a lack of compassion for themselves and others. When left unaddressed, individuals tend to self-sabotage, often inadvertently reliving their past damaging experiences in their present lives. This results in individuals closing themselves off, thinking and acting negatively, and limiting communication with others. Trauma is a natural aspect of life, but when individuals become stuck in a cycle of traumatic experiences, it can feel like an ongoing, inescapable ordeal.

When our body becomes used to reacting to real danger, it will respond as intensely for any perceived risk, which limits the body's ability to face and overcome obstacles or hardships (no matter how small) in daily life. You may find yourself responding aggressively to arguments, or you may avoid unfamiliar tasks, even if they are important. Or you might turn to different forms of distraction to avoid your problems. If you're stuck in the trauma cycle, you may be unable to admit any wrongdoing or vulnerability, and you'll do anything possible to avoid the difficult emotions that accompanied the biggest upheaval of your life. We stop knowing truth versus fiction in life because we interpret every situation as though it has the potential to be as terrifying as our past traumas, even if we logically know we are safe.

As you endeavor to reconcile past traumas, it is important to remember that healing is not a solitary endeavor. It thrives within a framework of vital social, cultural, and relational support systems. While applying healing tools and practices, it is important to surround ourselves with genuine friends, family, and community networks that can provide the understanding and encouragement necessary for navigating this complex process. These connections create a safety net that facilitates vulnerability and shared healing. When we start to follow pathways of healing, we will inevitably face brutal truths about ourselves and our pasts. However, by intentionally engaging with our history and fostering supportive relationships with ourselves and others, we open the possibility for transformation and renewal in our lives to flow authentically.

On the other hand, failing to heal from traumatic damage will eventually lead to detachment from one's authentic self. Because of an unwillingness to approach healing authentically, many immigrants feel long-lasting effects of past trauma and displacement. Although trauma is a fact of life, traumatic injuries do not have to become lifelong burdens for wounded individuals, families, and traumatized cultural groups.

Central Healing Foundations

Through my personal work to overcome the trauma of rootlessness, and my professional work as a marriage and family therapist, I have created a model for healing trauma and cultural rootlessness called the **Four Central Healing Foundations**, which I often refer to as the Four C's. These are four important mental functions that our trauma interferes with—the four areas we must focus on in the pursuit of healing. These mental functions not only protect us, they help us grow and connect with others who are also on their own journeys. Their transformative power makes them foundational to healing.

The first mental foundation is **curiosity**, which works in conjunction with the brain. While all four of the central healing foundations rely on the brain, curiosity is especially tied to neurological functions since it involves the will to learn. A healthy mind is inquisitive about ideas, people, the natural world, the past, and the future. Trauma interferes with our innate curiosity by either telling us that the world is too dangerous to explore, or forcing us into more and more unwanted or undesired situations to distract ourselves from feeling difficult emotions. Curiosity is a central healing foundation when it helps us listen to our true intuition (not our fears) and become interested in new experiences and people that are good for us. Developing, or rediscovering, curiosity often means relying on your faith or system of belief, those whom you trust as wise counsel, or resources like this book to provide emotional support while you follow your curiosity and become more open to the world around you.

The second mental foundation is **compassion**, which works with the symbolic heart. While the other "C's" are also linked to the heart, compassion is especially heart-centered and heart-focused. We must use compassion as a vehicle to nurture, care for, and love ourselves. When we are in the trauma cycle, we judge ourselves and others harshly because we feel that any mistake could lead to danger. In the trauma cycle, we don't trust the world around us, and we lack a belief in our capabilities to develop healthy relationships with ourselves and others. As a mental foundation, compassion allows us and those around us the safety to make mistakes and face difficulties with unconditional nurturance, care, and loving support. Without it, we are easily overwhelmed. If we are too judgmental or harsh with ourselves, we can't reap the benefits of the work that we are seeking for healing and growth.

The third mental foundation is **creativity**, which is symbolized through the spirit, whom many people think of as the ultimate "creator." Creativity relates to the tools and approaches we can use to live a healthier lifestyle. When we are stuck in a mental or emotional rut, creative thinking can help us envision a way beyond our current circumstances. Creativity moves us to take healthy risks outside of repeated painful thoughts and behaviors, and it empowers us to imagine the life we want to eventually live. Creativity is a powerful function because it challenges feelings of worthlessness. As a mental function, creativity requires that we confront our lives with honest eyes and assess what could be different.

The fourth mental foundation is **courage**, which is symbolized through attitude. Courage can be represented by having patience with your unique life path. Faith or a system of belief can support this patience. It is also critical that we courageously acknowledge that we can persist through pain. We all have the ability to bravely reinterpret trauma as something that will end—something we can move past and grow from in myriad ways. We must see loving ourselves as a number one priority, not an optional luxury that only appears when convenient. Often, anxiety, depression, and other illnesses can take away our confidence to courageously walk through life with authentic faith, beliefs, and value practices. However, when we believe that it is indeed a personal responsibility to love ourselves, we adjust the way we think, behave, and talk. Courage, as a mental foundation, gives people the power to honor themselves and their dreams through action.

Put together, these Four Central Healing Foundations remind us that, regardless of our cultural trauma or rootlessness, we come from our creator, who naturally gifts us the internal thinking powers to rebuild our external dream lives fully. The four healing foundations empower us to achieve greatness, and they form an interlocking web of possibility, each one strengthened by the rest.

The following chapters will include more details about these functions and explain how each of them is rooted in scientific and physiological realities. Each foundation is connected to self-mastery, which will empower you to become rooted in a journey of restoration, transformation, growth, and healing.

CHAPTER 3

THE CURIOUS MIND AND SELF-EXPLORATION

The first mental foundation is curiosity, which works in conjunction with the brain. When we are stuck in a pattern of unhelpful thoughts and behaviors, our curiosity can act as a flashlight to illuminate possibilities to help us find pathways to exit the trauma cycle.

In this context, curiosity makes us conscious of how our minds work, so we can regain control of our thoughts. It is essential to remember that our lives are made up of interactions between our minds, bodies, and the world around us. The human brain works through communication networks which allow parts of our brain to "talk" to each other and work together to control bodily functions, emotions, thinking, behavior, and everything else we do. To save energy, our brain appreciates familiarity and tries to recognize patterns as often as possible to process what's happening around us. For those who have endured traumatic experiences, the brain may develop thought patterns that signal danger or potential harm, even in nonthreatening situations.

However, the brain is adaptive and can learn new habits and patterns. Its adaptability is called neuroplasticity. In simple terms, the idea of neuroplasticity suggests that we can create new patterns for the brain to react to difficult or tough situations. To build new patterns that better fit our current life situations, we must become curious about what those current patterns look like, so we can recognize and potentially change them.

A lack of curiosity may signal underlying depression, which could stem from unhealed traumatic damages or feeling rootless. The symptoms of depression are manyfold, but they could manifest in a loss of interest in regular daily activities, feelings of conditioned hopelessness, helplessness, worthlessness, shame, guilt, fatigue, poor self-image, problems with food, excessive weight loss or weight gain, sleep problems, low self-esteem, repeated negative talk and behaviors, angry outbursts, poor impulse control, and/or lower desires or passion to live, as well as suicidal or homicidal ideations and self-injurious behaviors with or without intent, plans, or means to harm oneself or others. For anyone experiencing the last few symptoms in the list, it is imperative to undergo a comprehensive safety risk assessment to evaluate imminent dangers, and to help a professional or provider respond more effectively and accurately. My primary, unconditional goal (and the goal of most therapists) is to provide therapeutic services, resources, and support that consistently aim to keep the individual, couples, family, and cultural and community group members safe. Other symptoms of trauma-induced depression include mood swings, persistent sadness, self-isolation, repetitive negative thoughts, poor communication, behavioral issues, neglect of self-care, reluctance to embrace change, and persistent fear, as well as a lack of motivation and willingness to enrich life through new experiences. All these symptoms are often informed by unhealed past traumas. Whether conscious or not, a past trauma might make a person feel that they are unworthy of self-care or that it isn't worth it to be curious and try new things since more pain will come anyway. These are examples of thought patterns informed by trauma that can keep someone in a state of fear and pain, unable to explore their interests or move forward.

Moving Past Trauma Through Curiosity

To take steps to move past trauma and overcome a stagnant or depressive state of mind, we must routinely be intentionally inquisitive about our ideas, thoughts, self-image, habits, past, and wishes for the future. Curiosity is a way to think with more openness and to develop conscious thought patterns. If we keep curious, it is possible to learn new lessons from the past which we can apply to our present-day selves. In my practice as a therapist, I utilize a cognitive and narrative therapy approach through open-ended questions, starting with the following:

- Who were you in the past or during childhood?
- What are the primary challenges in your life today?
- How do these challenges presently impact your life and your ability to live a better quality of life? (For example, do you find yourself often thinking negatively about yourself or having more positive thoughts about yourself?)
- Do you often behave in aggressive, hostile, or angry ways toward others?

I then ask the patient for specific examples. The origin of their negative patterns often comes out in these stories, yet these stories can also contain the keys to healing.

After my clients reflect on their challenges, I have them reevaluate those difficult times from their past to identify ways they have tried to protect themselves and move through their problems. Some of my follow-up questions might include:

- What strengths do you display when dealing with your challenges?
- What healing tools have you already tried, and how have they worked for you?
- How could you start thinking about your past experiences in ways that motivate you to better nurture, care for, and love the person you are today?

After considering your trauma, how you've processed it, and how you are thinking about it presently, the next logical step is to practice reframing your thoughts and speech (which can eventually lead to reframing actions and behaviors). I encourage my clients to move from absolute statements ("I cannot," "I will not," or "Things never work out for me") toward a more flexible perspective ("I am willing to try my best, slowly"). Simply reframing self-talk can open a person's viewpoint and enable curiosity.

If the shifts you want in life seem unattainable, start by becoming curious about your own mental patterns. The brain serves as a container for negative thought patterns programmed by unresolved traumas, and the initial healing stages focus on the healer getting to know their thinking brain daily. You may find that you automatically shut yourself down or dig in your heels, mechanisms for protecting yourself from future disappointments. When my clients consistently reflect on their thought patterns and intentionally work on expanding their trust, faith, and personal beliefs, I usually see their behaviors eventually begin to match their curiosity. Curiosity is a critical process because what is true to us will determine how we choose to interact with ourselves, family members, spirituality, and community.

Our curious mind is the first supportive network we must reclaim along the four central healing pathways to create an authentic self and lifestyle. The curious mind determines how a person can change and move past trauma. It is important to reflect on negative or positive aspects or changes we notice in ourselves, in addition to recognizing our perspectives. Since we are always perceiving things, we are always changing.

Additionally, being curious requires that we push the mind to realize that something unexpected may happen to the body, and come to terms with it. Refugees may develop a deep-seated fear of the unknown, so becoming curious and accepting new experiences and events is a major step forward.

Curiosity in Action

Change can become more welcomed and controlled by the conscious mind through more self-aware practices. Genuine thoughtfulness requires an open mind, not an adherence to fixed ideas. Investing in an open-minded and tolerant attitude to accurately interpret, reflect on, and shape understandings of our experiences is critical. Constantly asking questions and having an inquisitive attitude can help us better understand the culture and ever-changing world unfolding around us.

This attitude also relates to cultural rootlessness. When we choose to be curious, we start to think about how life might be if we either embrace or reject certain elements of our past and present. On the one hand, we might find comfort and community in our heritage (enjoying traditional meals, speaking our ancestors' language, upholding specific customs), but certain elements of our heritage may no longer serve us. For example, arranged marriages are common in Liberia. Therefore, when my parents found me a marriage match, I did not resist. I met my wife in person for the first time four days before our wedding, when we vowed to spend our lives together. Unfortunately, this tradition did not serve us, and several years later we ended up filing for divorce.

This example highlights my lack of curiosity in this situation. I decided to acquiesce to my parents' wishes without being curious and asking, "What if?" What if I decided to say no? What if I opted to go down a different path? It is important to know that rooting yourself in your culture does *not* mean blindly embracing it. It is okay to question certain aspects of your culture and carve your own path forward, rooting yourself in truth and authenticity.

An inquisitive attitude can also help us explore trauma and past life events with greater openness. The life you are working on is complicated to achieve. Your trauma can be deeply connected to your land of origin and culture, influencing how you think about them (causing some to wholly reject their culture, when that is not necessarily the best course of action). In exploring the therapeutic process, we must acknowledge our cultural heritage as we work toward better lives, recognizing that some aspects of our heritage can, indeed, be healing and affirming.

When adapting a mindset of curiosity, it is important to recognize any negative beliefs you have about yourself and your present environment. Then, consider the advice of those who have helped you through tough environments. Engage in honest self-reflection and be willing to consider new ideas. You may find that you no longer identify with core beliefs about yourself, or that parts of your identity have become uncomfortable to think about for any number of reasons. Then, you can consciously decide if your beliefs and associations are true for you. This is the essence of curious thinking.

My Early Experiences with Inquisitive Thinking

When I first arrived in the United States, I had to put my curious mind to work. The transition to the United States was treacherous. When I landed at JFK Airport in New York City, the landscape was clustered with so many skyscrapers, I could barely wrap my head around their presence. My uncle—an important figure in those first weeks—picked us up from the airport and took us to his home. Like my dad, my uncle had already established himself in the United States, settling in Trenton, New Jersey, where there is a big Liberian population. One of our first meals was at Burger King. Though the food was new, I kept my curious mind open and gave it a shot. Unfortunately, I threw up after a few bites, an apt metaphor for how overwhelmed my system was by the move from Liberia to the United States. However, that didn't stop me from staying curious and continuing to try American food.

In the United States, I wrestled constantly with my past, not wanting to relive the trauma inflicted by the civil war. I was so triggered, I would avoid anything that reminded me of the war, such as loud fireworks on Independence Day. The first time I heard a loud bang, I thought it was a gun. I also shied away from new friendships because I struggled to trust people, and I feared vulnerability. Living in war-torn Liberia taught me not to trust anyone outside my immediate family and community. We survived by closing ourselves off from others. Thus, meeting new people and forming new friendships in the United States felt vaguely threatening. Interacting with unknown people brought back memories of the war in Liberia, where my safety was constantly at risk. Because of these deep-seated fears, one of my biggest challenges was to learn how to trust others, live in the present, and not think of survival.

Fortunately, I was able to find some support. I lived in a cabin with my mother, father, and sister in the Iowa countryside. We were taken in by a wonderful US family that always compassionately supported my Liberian family and me. Dan, Margaret, Nate, and Sam are amazing people who took us in and supported us. Dan was the first to put a basketball in my hands, and I fondly remember playing "pig" and "horse" with his son Nate and the other kids living next door. I had beautiful experiences in rural Iowa—riding bikes with Nate, picking fruit from trees (we lived near an apple farm), eating dinner together, and experiencing life without civil war for the first time. They say it takes a village to raise a child, and I have found that to be true. When trauma tarnishes your life, parental guidance, love, community, and family support are an oasis. Without this oasis, curiosity is nearly impossible.

Although I did not realize it, these simple moments in Iowa served as seeds to develop my therapeutic philosophy of the Four C's, the cornerstones of healing from trauma: curiosity, compassion, creativity, and courage. To live our best curious, compassionate, creative, and courageous lives, we must heal past wounds in present spaces and slowly be open to relational change, communal shifts, and mental, physical, and sociocultural discomfort in the United States. We must establish our own roots—a mix of cultural heritage and new ways of thinking and doing. We all deserve to live our best lives, and that can often be realized in strange ways. However, with trust, we can become the best versions of ourselves, even if the path is difficult to see at first. Embracing authentic care, and receiving love from myself and others, has taught me this.

When I moved to Iowa City, I found support and positivity from a variety of people and places. I had a couple of friends in the neighborhood, and I would ride bikes all day with my Filipino friend, Barka, and my Puerto Rican friend, Roberto. In Mark Twain Elementary School, I found guidance from a fourth-grade teacher, who helped me tremendously. At lunch time, she would sit with me and read, and she would use her extra time to take me to the library. This personal attention built my confidence and sense of self, which allowed me to be curious about what I was learning and the new environment in which I found myself. The healing power of the energy my Iowa City community poured into me cannot be overstated. This, despite most people not knowing my ethnicity or understanding the baggage I was carrying. Above all, I began to realize that community can be chosen anywhere when we begin to understand ourselves.

While I was not completely privy to this wisdom as a child, I was starting to learn it as I was forced to adapt to US society and cultural norms. Even with support, I couldn't release the knowledge of the war and was always anxious, waiting for something to go wrong. I would often look over my shoulder because I didn't like my back exposed to doors. I would incessantly check to see if doors were locked behind me. At random times, my heart would start racing, my internal wiring telling me to fight or flee, and I quickly had to learn how to deescalate. I was beginning to learn that I had to accept the adage, "Where you go, you take you with you." My journey in Iowa required me to confront this reality in a very difficult way. It was a message that would be hard to hold onto as my life progressed.

For example, I used to think I would fail my tests in college, even after preparing and studying. With my thoughts hyper-focused on failing and my mind muddled, this became a self-fulfilling prophecy, and I often *did* fail or received a barely passing grade. Sometimes, the professors would go over the results with me and say, "Why do you know the correct answers now, but you got them wrong on the test?" I came to realize my negative thinking was reducing my confidence, turning my knowledge and understanding into fear of failure. On one test, I intentionally worked on applying curiosity-related thinking patterns. What I mean by this is that I opened myself to thinking differently—to becoming curious about alternative ways to learn and retain information. My curiosity led me to study differently than most, using visual and auditory aids, such as videos and recorded materials, to prepare for the test. Able to retain the information more effectively, I received a better passing score, one of the highest scores in the class. With a more open and clear mind, improved confidence, and the ability to adapt to unforeseen challenges, I opened myself to making improvements.

We must first work on changing our mentalities—then we can slowly work on changing our behaviors. Thinking holds the power to drive communication, feelings or emotions, beliefs, faith, motivations, and behaviors. Thinking or being willing to think in more open-minded ways empowers more open-minded interactions and authentic behaviors to flow, improving our chances to thrive. On the other hand, remaining closed-minded and frightened will always restrict and limit our chances to overcome our damages. It's important to remind ourselves, no matter our experiences, that we always hold the power to decide how we want to think. Curious thinking aims to eventually get the mind and body working together authentically, meaning our thinking and behaviors match our desired perspectives and lifestyles.

REFLECTION QUESTIONS

Get CURIOUS about your past. As you develop your healing path, ask yourself about your roots. Jot down your thoughts in a notebook if you'd like, and revisit these questions whenever you need.

1. What important personal details do you use to define yourself?
2. How do your birth time and place impact your life's journey?
3. How has your race impacted the way you are perceived or the way you engage with the world?
4. Which dominant cultures likely informed your identity?
5. What habits, heritage, and tribal bonds have you inherited?
6. How do you understand "Western Civilization" and its relationship to your identity formation?
7. Where did you come from initially? (Historically, where did your lineage or heritage live? Whether known or unknown, I encourage you to also explore other cultural or diverse aspects of your childhood that you want to reconnect with on a deeper level.)
8. What happened to you during childhood that you believe negatively affects you in your present environment?
9. What does cultural healing mean to you?
10. Who taught you how to nurture, care, and love yourself? How do the patterns of nurturing, caring, and loving that you experienced in childhood impact your life today? How could you continue to improve your ability to nurture, care for, and show love to yourself and others?
11. What caused you to leave your country?

CHAPTER
4

THE COMPASSIONATE HEART AND SELF-DISCOVERY

The second mental foundation is compassion, which works in conjunction with the heart. We often absorb the natural feelings and emotions of the people closest to us without question, especially when we've been traumatized. The self-compassionate heart helps us love and protect ourselves without feeling others' depression, frustration, or anxiety as though it were our own. The practice of self-compassion is our ability to apply unconditional self-love to mental, emotional, and behavioral patterns. A compassionate heart functions without fears, judgments, blame, and hatred. When we tap into this compassion and start treating ourselves with more tenderness, we realize that we have a fundamental ability to care for ourselves and love our wounds.

Through our compassionate heart, we can thrive no matter our circumstances. For many, compassion may be a code word for gentleness. This is ironic, because it is through gentleness (and compassion) that we can become stronger. When we pair gentleness with honesty or candidness, it is possible to enact change. In truth, gentleness and honesty are not two opposing forces. We can be honest with ourselves about where we are in our lives, while also being gentle with where we desire to go. This is what I call "radical honesty." By exhibiting radical honesty, we can move beyond the damage of our traumas and learn who we can truly be.

Each and every immigrant should be empowered to walk through their journey with compassion, honesty, and gentleness.

We may often feel as though we don't deserve our own compassion, but this certainly is not the case. Our unique storylines and lived circumstances require that we slow down and pause, taking our trauma day by day. When you've lived through traumatic situations, it's likely that you've responded in ways you're not proud of. Some people even believe that their life choices caused them to deserve their trauma, which is a story that allows them to feel more in control of their lives. Self-compassion means accepting that we are not primarily "bad" or "good," but that we are all capable of making good or bad choices under certain circumstances. When we think of ourselves compassionately, we can see our flaws and the conditions that created them without placing blame. We may regret choices we've made, but it is not productive to endlessly punish ourselves for them. We can see the past for how it shaped us while allowing ourselves to move forward. It is through these authentic reflections that we can find the compassion we need for ourselves and also apply it to others in our community.

When we pair self-compassion with honesty and authenticity, we can start to acknowledge our struggles and put ourselves in a healing frame of mind. Part of this work involves trusting our internal compass (our human soul), which was made to help us solve problems. When you trust your inner wisdom, incredible transformations are possible.

Compassion and Comparisons

Those who are displaced and come from immigrant or refugee backgrounds are often in a constant fight for survival, whether real or imagined. Our experiences make us vulnerable, and we may feel that we lack physical and/or emotional protection. This is an unnatural and difficult way of living. While we are often far removed from the experiences of anguish in our home countries—civil war, violence in communities, traumas from early childhood, tribal trauma, homelessness and poverty, or abuse—we still carry these things with us. It is not enough to believe that they disappear at the border when we emigrate. Since these experiences stay with us, it is important to consider how to be compassionate to ourselves within this context, even if, on the surface, our new country seems "better."

Many of us might feel guilty about still feeling as though we are on a healing journey, even though we've arrived in a land of opportunity (compared to one's country of origin, where those who were left behind may still be suffering). We may also compare ourselves with others—those in our homeland, as well as the people in our adopted country. Comparing yourself to others often leads to negative emotions like jealousy and anger, distracting you from living a fulfilled life. Since everyone's experiences and circumstances are vastly different, this tendency to constantly judge and compare is not productive. Rather than dwelling on what you (or others) lack, it is far better to practice gratitude and compassion. Make an effort to appreciate things like family, friends, and the everyday joys of life. Make it a habit to list what you are thankful for daily or weekly. Being compassionate toward yourself and others can free you from the chains of comparison.

Learning to love and appreciate yourself is crucial, regardless of your achievements or setbacks. Compassion allows us to acknowledge life's complexities and strive for positive changes. It is about treating yourself and others with kindness and love, regardless of external or social differences. Ultimately, everyone deserves love and compassion, no matter their past actions, background, or current circumstances.

I had to relearn how to love myself and show compassion to my body during my healing journey. When I was in pain, I would compare myself to others, leading to low self-esteem, low-confidence, sadness, confusion, poor self-worth, shame, guilt, regret, excessive worry, and neglect of my spiritual, mental and emotional health. It was not until I started learning to fully love myself and accept all my qualities that things began to change. I did this through consistent prayers, asking for support from my spiritual higher power (Lord-God), positive self-talk behaviors, and changing my thought patterns from judging and comparing to compassion. I became more willing to see my life as valuable, even before I was thriving in my new society and making material gains. We can all return to a more compassionate state by learning to care for, nurture, and love ourselves and others unconditionally, regardless of our differences. We must minimize comparison and judgment and promote acceptance, support, and nonjudgmental behaviors.

Another reason comparison is harmful is that it can lead to feelings of entitlement ("I *deserve* what others have"), often leaving us feeling incomplete. When we compare ourselves to others, we start to believe we must continually improve, regardless of our achievements. Entitlement causes us to compare our achievements to others, provoking envy and hindering us from focusing on our meaningful goals. It keeps us stuck in jobs, relationships, or experiences that aren't good for us because we grow so attached to the idea of reaching milestones defined by others, rather than paying attention to our own reality and needs—the healthy situations we need to flow into our lives without judgments or comparison. This sense of entitlement can distract us from appreciating life's essential aspects, such as family, friends, loved ones, and the fact that we are alive and breathing today. Feeling entitled drains our energy and motivation because nothing meets our ever-changing desires.

On the other hand, gratitude and thankfulness can allow us to be happy with our present state. We tend to feel better in our daily activities when we are grateful, and this mindset helps us to genuinely focus on ourselves, accept others, overcome the urge to stop comparing, and accept changes to move through life without judgment. We can stop the endless comparison cycle when we learn to love ourselves and appreciate our uniqueness authentically.

Confronting (and Ignoring) Struggles

On our journey of self-love and compassion, we must be careful not to minimize our struggles. Your struggles are valid, no matter how minor or major, trivial or significant, they may seem to others. We are all human beings, wired with a soul and spirit that deserve unconditional compassion, gentleness, empathy, and love. By affirming this, we can repair harm, acknowledge and overcome struggles, and accelerate the healing process.

By affirming the truth that we are all on a journey, no matter how good things may seem, we can acknowledge our personal recovery process and reimagine it. We also can challenge negative attitudes, false opinions, and others' beliefs that we may have absorbed along the way. Compassion enables the mind and body to be flexible enough to manage the repercussions of cultural displacement and rootlessness. Compassion is how we get our mind and body to agree to heal. We must remember that our self-compassion must be unconditional. Much like the love of a long-term partner, the compassion we give ourselves cannot be dependent upon how perfect we are. We will inevitably fail on our journeys many times over, but that does not mean we do not deserve compassion. Our self-compassion should be endless and abundant, especially in a world where others will not always grant it to us. The last thing that anybody who has survived trauma needs is another negative voice or mindset creeping in their psyche.

Compassion is something I had to learn through my own journey as a high school and college basketball player. For years, basketball was an outlet for me to find community, take ownership of a path forward, and build confidence. When I felt like I had nothing, I at least had basketball. Basketball was a language of its own that I could use to speak to people from all over the country. At any court or gym, I became in sync with my adopted society. This offered me much-needed comfort as I struggled to resolve how different my environment was from my home country of Liberia. Basketball brought me joy, mentorship, and camaraderie. However, basketball also brought me distraction.

Over time, I realized that, although it brought me comfort, I was using basketball as an escape. I would play for hours on any given day and became quite obsessed, fleeing from my problems, insecurities, and struggles. While this seemed like a productive activity to those on the outside, it was something that created a lot of pressure in me as time went on, especially toward the end of high school. Since basketball was a potential ticket to higher education, many people had expectations for me to perform well and earn a scholarship. For my immigrant parents, this was a huge opportunity that I could not afford to waste. I internalized the pressure and worked hard to succeed at the game of basketball, despite my uneasiness about the academic difficulties I was facing and my feelings of isolation and dissonance in the United States. The pressure was extremely hard to explain to those who could not understand how a seemingly perfect immigrant story was going wrong.

If I had taken the time to confront my struggles, I might have been able to deal with all the pressure on my shoulders. At this point in my life, however, I had not taken the time to engage in meaningful reflection or conversation, therapy, or the difficult work of reconciling my past with my present. I had not dared to fully face my struggles with academics, friendships and other relationships, or feeling like a fish out of water in certain social situations. Because I had not compassionately confronted my struggles, I paid the price.

The Consequences of Burying Trauma

Eventually, I began to cope with the overwhelming pressure to perform well in basketball by turning to alcohol. If you know anyone who abuses alcohol, you know that it can be very addictive and is also something that people can hide. I had become extremely good at hiding what I was enduring and burying my inner turmoil with alcohol. Though on the surface I seemed to be thriving, "all that glitters is not gold." I was not granting myself the compassion necessary to realize that I had several deep issues and traumas that were unresolved, and I felt like I had no one to turn to. So, I turned to the bottle as a container for my pain, despite the harm it caused me in return.

My alcohol dependence impacted my relationships, my academic pursuits, and, ultimately, my health. I used to drink heavily to alleviate the pain of comparison—the need to be like others and fit in. Many immigrants can likely relate to this sentiment. We often seem out of place, caught between two different cultures and feeling like we're not thriving in either of them. In my case, I lacked self-love and constantly sought validation from others, making me want to excel and seek acceptance. Internally, I grappled with low self-esteem, negative self-beliefs, and a shaky sense of identity, prioritizing others' perceptions of me over my own. Unfortunately, this also led me to compare my alcohol consumption to that of my peers.

I used to constantly worry about disappointing my parents. This deeply held fear led me to seek solace in alcohol as a means of escaping the stress. Initially, I drank to momentarily pause the overwhelming pressure I felt. However, this tendency soon spiraled out of control. Alcohol became my refuge, a way to distance myself from my parents, old wounds, friends, and the sport I once loved. It became my self-contained world, and I was oblivious to its detrimental effects, focusing only on the temporary relief it provided every time I drank. Though it did not truly relax me, it managed to numb the pain and provide a fleeting escape from the realities of basketball, school, relationships, and whatever difficulties I was experiencing in the present moment. Sadly, this false comfort only fueled my desire to continue this harmful behavior. I know other immigrants can relate to this type of impulse—the desire to put a Band-Aid on your wound, rather than truly treating and healing it. It's human nature to head down the path of least resistance, even if that path will only lead to a temporary relief of pain and further hardships down the road. We choose momentary relief over the painful work of confronting our struggles with compassion and self-love.

Looking back on my era of alcohol abuse, I understand why my environment led me to seek unhealthy escapes. I struggled with low self-esteem and repetitive negative thoughts about being at a prestigious college. I also felt culturally disconnected from my friends and the student community because there were very few Liberians on campus. To break through these barriers, I developed a dependence on alcohol. When I was sober, I felt shy and self-conscious, but when I was drinking, I felt more confident and able to communicate and socialize, especially with women. I also used it as an escape from trauma, turning fears into false confidence, sadness into fleeting laughter, and pain into numbness.

As a young person, I chased these urges and sensations; the drinking could take me to a world where I felt special.

However, social drinking turned into isolation, with me often drinking by myself either during the day or at night. The drinking replaced the validation and acceptance I felt on the basketball court. Eventually, I wanted to drink alcohol more than I wanted to play basketball, and it did not matter if I drank alone or with others. Once I was drinking, I felt like the reality I had lived, and my present challenges in school, were distant and imaginary. It gave me the power to create and live in a new reality. Although unhealthy, I constantly convinced myself that this state of being was beautiful, ignoring any painful consequences, breakups, injuries, and academic punishments.

I was solely focused on the immediate pleasure that the bottle provided. I felt disconnected from my true self and struggled to understand where my life was headed. Witnessing my peers and basketball teammates' confidence about their plans after college was tough, and I felt lost. When I compared myself with them—their effortless confidence, their ability to fit in, and the way they seemingly had it all figured out—I felt inadequate and my sadness deepened. Alcohol became a battleground for me because I had not yet confronted and healed from the emotional scars of my past. Drinking became a coping mechanism, a way to temporarily escape the emotional turmoil caused by my experiences in Liberia and the United States. Despite the physical discomfort it sometimes brought, alcohol seemed like a better alternative to facing the pain of my past. It became a constant companion, dulling the sharp edges of my memories and offering a reprieve from the inner turmoil. Eventually, it became a habit, a part of daily life. I couldn't control my need to escape, even though I knew it was wrong and hid it from my girlfriend.

Typically, I would start drinking as soon as basketball games ended. I would drink before class too, and my classmates often knew it. One time, I took six shots before an 8:00 a.m. Norwegian class. Alcohol is a depressant, and when my drinking got heavy, I would call my parents and text my friends things that they would ask me about later. Sometimes I couldn't even remember what I'd said. I tried therapy, but I didn't want to talk. I often left those sessions to drink.

This culminated in my senior year of undergraduate education. I was attending St. Olaf College, and, while I was supported enough in this environment to successfully complete four years of school while playing basketball, my journey took a tragic turn at the end of my senior year because of my personal struggles. I was hospitalized, not for a bone fracture or cardiac issue, but for alcohol poisoning. The day I was hospitalized was a "good" day. Our basketball team was a top-three seed. I woke up in the hospital, shocked and embarrassed that my issues had overcome me in such an apparent way. My parents were crying, and the university deans were at my bedside. They all gave me a second chance.

I was at my lowest. I couldn't compete in the playoffs, and the team said a prayer for me before their next game. I had to watch my team lose from home, thinking about how I had been a key player for the team earlier in the season. While finishing school that year, I had to stand in my shame. However, I decided to own my reconciliation as I embarked on my healing journey. Basketball, my ideal tool for escapism, was no longer sufficient. I needed to tell the truth about what I had carried across my life's journey and how it was evolving, for better or worse.

This is a lesson that anyone dealing with trauma should internalize: escapism is temporary, and your trauma will catch up with you eventually. My hope is that you will not have to hit rock bottom, as I did, to learn this lesson. Instead, I urge you to be intentional about your healing journey. Show yourself the compassion and respect you deserve by seeking the appropriate help and resources to unpack your trauma, learn from it, and heal.

Seeking Your Compassionate Community

Your efforts to heal from and overcome trauma will inevitably be more successful if you are supported by others. As you learn to love yourself unconditionally, it is important to seek that same kind of unwavering support from other people. Find friends, family members, mentors, and community members who will stick with you through good times and bad, through calm waters and stormy seas. At the same time, it is important to show this type of unconditional love and compassion to those around you. Be a true, steadfast friend, and you'll find that at least some people will return this authenticity and steadfastness. And if friendship isn't truly returned, honor yourself by limiting your exposure to fair-weather friends, who are only willing to stick around when times are good and you're feeling happy.

In the aftermath of my hospitalization from alcohol poisoning, I underwent a journey of personal growth and reconciliation by accepting support from my ex-girlfriend and fellow student, Leah. Throughout this process, I had to relearn how to establish a trustworthy friendship without the intimate aspect of our previous relationship. I also had to develop the confidence to communicate openly and honestly. As Leah continued to accept me without passing judgment, I found myself also becoming more open and accepting of others. I began to lower my defenses and open myself to verbal and physical interactions with others—interactions that were genuine, heartfelt, and free from the influence of alcohol.

Through Leah's unwavering support and love as a friend, I came to understand that I am worthy of love, even in moments of shame. I also learned that it is okay to be vulnerable, seek help, and receive support from others. We all experience pain and suffering at some point, and everyone deserves love through genuine friendships, family relationships, or partnerships. Relationships are crucial in healing, and we cannot overcome our struggles alone. We must cultivate authentic and functional relationships and support networks to guide us during difficult times—by both giving and receiving unwavering love and support. Nurturing, caring for, and loving one another unconditionally fuels us in our healing journeys.

My experience with alcohol abuse and recovery allowed me to gradually rebuild trust in myself and others, setting the stage for healthier interactions within my St. Olaf College community and among my basketball teammates. In turn, I wanted to help other people too.

However, not everyone was supportive and kind. I could walk

around campus and feel people talking about my alcohol abuse. When everything went south, I learned that people don't want to stand in the shame with you, but they *will* walk alongside you down the path leading to your downfall. Only a few peers—along with my parents, deans, and basketball coaches—stood by me during this difficult time. Before the incident, I used to hang out with many friends who would drink and party with me, and we would frequently text each other. But after the hospital incident, I stopped receiving text messages, and many people I used to hang out with no longer communicated with me. While on campus, no longer drinking and feeling hurt, only a few friends remained steadfast and would eat meals with me. I felt like an outcast, the basketball player with a drinking problem, who was no longer seen as excellent to be around. I began to understand the fickle nature of people. Most do not want to support others during hard times, opting to only stand with them during good times and triumphant moments. It is important to be clear-headed enough to see these people for who they are *and* to identify true friends and supporters when they enter your life. Hold the second group close and treat them like gold, because they are valuable beyond measure.

Through my experience, I have found peace by learning to love myself again and knowing that my higher power unconditionally loves me. I have learned to forgive my past, and through this forgiveness, I can now live free from its pain. I have also realized that transformation is possible for everyone.

After the incident, regardless of who remained close to me or didn't, or who judged me or didn't, I knew I had to become relentless about offering myself compassion. After leaving the hospital, embracing self-compassion was enormously challenging. I worried about my future in school, basketball, and facing my parents again. I felt much shame every day, isolated myself, and tried to avoid discussing the hospital situation. My parents were upset. In my senior year, I missed the playoffs due to injury, and the pain I felt was only compounded by my struggles with drinking, mental health, and unresolved cultural and traumatic issues. I temporarily moved off campus to my parents' apartment in

Bloomington, Minnesota, and they started driving me back and forth from Bloomington to Northfield for classes.

Overcoming shame was a slow process. My family and true friends checked in on me regularly, reminding me that I was still part of the St. Olaf community. Their kind words helped me realize it is okay to practice self-compassion. Believing I deserved love and care, I learned to love myself again. My parents and family stood by me, adjusting their schedules to support me. They taught me the power of compassion and love. Their unwavering support showed me that love does not have to fade, even in difficult times.

It is okay for me, and for you, to learn to love ourselves again. The trauma I tried to dismiss had come to the surface in a way that I could survive, but that I inevitably had to confront. Unresolved pain stays with us whether we want to think about it or not. Many of us are taught to be strong, push our emotions down, and pretend we are okay for the sake of ourselves and our families. This, however, is unproductive and does nothing to resolve trauma. Though it can be difficult and painful, it is essential to face your fears head-on to move forward in life. It was the compassion I had for myself, and from those who loved me, that enabled and empowered me to leave a dark place and move into a space of light and transformation. While fear causes us to dissociate from our problems or adapt unhelpful behaviors to cope, self-compassion allows us to understand ourselves and tend to the root cause of our problems. Our focus shifts from blaming and distracting ourselves to leveraging gratitude and using our compassionate heart as a guiding tool and compass to continue life's journey.

REFLECTION QUESTIONS

Treat your present self with COMPASSION. Answer the following questions with self-love and understanding. Jot down your thoughts in a notebook if you'd like, and revisit these questions whenever you need.

1. How do you see yourself now? What are your core values, traditions, habits, beliefs, strengths, and weaknesses? How would you describe yourself in four words?
2. How do your past experiences shape present perceptions of self?
3. What is your true self? Do you feel like expressing this authentic version of yourself to others? Why or why not?
4. How could you start to see yourself differently? Moving forward, how can you match the life you dream of living?
5. Do you believe you belong to a genuine community? How do you define "genuine"?
6. What parts of your life do you perceive as beautiful?
7. What part do you play in the United States at present? Compose a narrative in one paragraph that shows yourself from every angle, inside and out. For example: *(Name), who is (age) years old, identifies as (race), is a member of (cultural groups), and adheres to (your traditional practices). They see their current community as (adjectives). In US society, they feel (emotions).*
8. What is your cultural rootlessness story? What happened to you in your homeland before coming to the United States? What traumatic experiences continue to show up and damage your body in the United States? Describe any parts of your body and life that remain wounded and unhealed from traumas, such as experiencing war, poverty, homelessness,

any form of abuse, hunger, intimate partner violence, racism, financial stressors or dilemmas, a lack of basic needs, limited resources, limited health care services, living in a high-crime community, bullying in school, limited academic support or resources, living in a refugee camp, or forced displacement from your childhood home or country.

9. What other unhealed damages, traumas, and pain still live within your family system, spiritual foundations, and communal memberships?
10. What do you stand for in society? What are your values?
11. What is your authentic self-identity? (Think of personal attributes such as courage, humility, or integrity.)

CHAPTER

5

THE CREATIVE SOUL AND SELF-CREATION

The third mental foundation is the creative soul, which enables self-creation. We are spiritual beings at our core, possessing the divine power to live our best lives in a diverse functioning human world and foster connections with our creator and each other. We are spiritual beings, each imbued with a profound divine power that allows us to navigate and thrive through the rich tapestry of human experiences. This spiritual essence empowers us to seek out and embrace the best versions of ourselves, ultimately leading to a more fulfilling and authentic life. In our journey, we cultivate deep connections with our creator and one another, fostering an environment of love, understanding, and community. By recognizing our shared spirituality, we can appreciate each individual's diverse perspectives and experiences, creating a harmonious world where connections flourish and we uplift one another on our paths. We can do magnificent things for our health and wellness when we affirm our ability to direct our course, to creatively use our resources, to form new mental pathways, and to lean into the people and environments that help us heal. We are not simply our past or present. We are evolving and dynamic beings that are constantly wrestling with who and what we want to be. However, to truly create our future selves, we have to be open to new ideas and perceptions about self, and embrace the life we honestly dream of living wholeheartedly.

Creation and creativity share the same root. When we endeavor to create a new life for ourselves—to follow a new path—that inevitably takes a healthy dose of creativity. We must dare to think in new, out-of-the-box ways. We must reject stale or tired ways of thinking and being that do not serve us and, instead, look for ways to reinvent ourselves to our liking *or* rethink our life's course. Whenever we have the courage to do something different, that takes creativity, and forging a new way forward (engaging in self-creation) is one of the most terrifying yet rewarding creative acts there is.

As immigrants to the United States, there is immense power in embracing the belief that who we are is changing rather than fixed. Oftentimes, we may feel as though our story has been written for us. Structural factors such as discrimination or other hardships are often a core part of our experiences in ways that can be hard to shake. However, we have the ultimate power to shape the way we perceive ourselves within the larger story of life. It is crucial to remember that despite the troubles we endure, we can belong and we can create new paths forward by tapping into our personal courage and the courage instilled in us from our higher spiritual power and communities. It is only after we use our license to create our own perspectives, outlooks, and worldviews that we can continue to heal from the traumas of our past.

Tapping Into Something Greater

We often underestimate the powerful roles our spirits and souls have in how we view our futures. I recognize that many may see the word "spirit" or "soul" and think of religion and faith-based systems. This framework might be relevant in some people's journeys when thinking about the possibilities of the soul, but others may not resonate with this link as much, depending on their backgrounds and perspectives. Regardless of your relationship with the words "soul" or "spirit," it is important to understand the meaning behind the concept. Ultimately, it is important to think about the sense of purpose that we all feel—the calling that goes beyond ourselves. When considering our purpose in life, we can tie that to the intentional act of reinventing or re-creating ourselves—the way we choose to step forward.

Sometimes, the consequences of living in a hyperindividualized society can impact the way we process trauma and healing. We forget that our problems, stories, and even triumphs are large to us but small in the scope of the universe. When we endeavor to think about our paths beyond personal experiences and move toward an idea of a spiritual experience, we can better understand the steps needed to move forward on a self-creation journey. Personally, I find solace in spirituality when dealing with trauma. Through prayer and reading the Bible, my trust in God helps me cope. I pray multiple times daily, expressing gratitude for each day and asking for healing for those in need. Attending church on Sundays is my way of finding peace and rest.

Reading the Bible and meditating on God's words and teachings have helped me build faith and trust in a higher power. I credit all my successes to my Heavenly Father and strive to live a truthful, humble life. Rediscovering my spirituality has led me to love and accept myself and others unconditionally, fostering humility and genuine compassion in my interactions with my creator, Jesus Christ, and the world more honestly and wholly. To God be the glory forever!

Alternatively, people can express their spirituality and humanity by donating their time and resources to those in need. This could include volunteering in the community for organizations that support others (Feed My Starving Children is one such organization that I wholeheartedly recommend). Support can also be provided through financial assistance, relational help, spiritual guidance, mentoring, or cultural resources (without expecting anything in return).

Additionally, individuals can demonstrate kindness and humanity by treating one another with compassion and meaning. This includes using kind words, respecting cultural differences, seeking to understand others rather than demanding to be understood, and practicing unconditional love for oneself and others.

Furthermore, people can embody spirituality by living honestly and avoiding deceit, lies, manipulation, and violence. Spirituality is fundamentally about loving our almighty Heavenly Father with all our heart, mind, and soul, and loving our neighbors as we love ourselves. Therefore, we should strive to lead lives encouraging us to love our neighbors, regardless of our differences.

Creating Your Own Future

Although we will go through trials and tribulations, we are more than our experiences. We are vessels that have the divine opportunity to reshape our perspectives and outlooks about the things that we've experienced. The most beautiful thing to remember, especially as an immigrant to the US experiencing cultural rootlessness, is that it is never too late to create one's future. This ability belongs to us all, at any given moment, despite the self-limiting beliefs we may hold. We are not damaged; we are dynamic. To operate from a place of our highest good, we must believe in the arc of redemption enough to tend to our special and unique needs and to use resources offered by those who care about us.

This attitude was something I had to learn once I graduated from my undergraduate studies at St. Olaf. I began work as a hall monitor at a high school and was just starting to digest and reflect on all the difficulties I had experienced with substance abuse and addiction. I had a long journey ahead of me, and I knew it, but it seemed I was only capable of putting one foot in front of the other. This left me feeling powerless, ashamed, and timid in ways that were unproductive for me as a young man embarking on his first steps as a full adult. My time working as a hall monitor at the high school was quite challenging. I often found it hard to assert my authority, as many students didn't care much about the rules, which seemed minor compared to the other issues they faced, such as poverty, homelessness, and behavioral problems. Encouraging them to attend classes was difficult. Some even refused to go, leading to interventions with the principal. I sometimes had to break up physical fights and manage disruptive behaviors in the classroom.

After these experiences, I realized I wanted to offer more compassionate support to students. Understanding their challenges, I knew they needed empathetic and relational support. This inspired me to pursue a career in mental health. Now, as a licensed marriage and family therapist, I aim to help others through compassion and collaboration.

One of the administrators at the school noticed my empathetic tendencies and talked to me about his observations. He said I needed to begin thinking about how I would use my social work degree, because I couldn't stay there forever. He didn't say this because he didn't like me as an employee, but rather to encourage me to use self-creation to continue to chart a path of purpose for myself. The administrator knew I wanted to help people, but he also knew I didn't know how I would embark on that journey. I considered this a huge turning point in my life, because he positioned himself as a mentor and encouraged me to tap into the traits and tendencies that were already embedded deep down within myself. Instead of giving me specific instructions or methods on how to live, he challenged me to think about what would feed my soul—my creative soul.

I had a few different mentors during this time, and not all of them were fully aware of the struggles I'd had at St. Olaf. However, I believe they all could tell I was driven by something. After feeling so isolated during my transition to the United States and persisting through addiction, I had become very sensitive to the presence, and sometimes absence, of relationships. I had become what I would call a relational person, deeply appreciating when I could tell that people cared about me. I also enjoyed showing up for others.

Relationships were something I began to love when I started playing basketball. I was the point guard of the team, one of the most important positions on the floor for holding a team together. I had to learn how to be vocal, communicate with people differently based on their needs, and maintain an overall vision for what a healthy unit could look like. My coach, much like the administrator at the high school, was instrumental in how I began to understand life and self-mastery.

In your own life, what are your interests and passions? What experiences have shaped your path or pointed you in a certain direction? If you're unsure, I encourage you to take a few minutes to ponder these questions. Everyone has interests or passions, but we do not always dare to pursue them. We might shuffle them off to the side for any number of reasons—family expectations, pressure from society or our peers, fear, the desire to make money. However, those interests are still there, and it is up to us to unearth them, embrace them, and figure out how to weave them into our lives. This could mean volunteering, picking up a new hobby, making a career change, or even making a major life alteration, such as moving to a new place or breaking off a harmful relationship.

In my case, my collection of experiences and mentorships led me to enroll in a master's program in marriage and family therapy. During my studies, I learned work-life balance and how to communicate with people across generations and backgrounds. I realized that we are all a sum of our experiences, and I took this as permission to lean into what made me different. I found my approach to counseling to be distinct from my classmates' approach, in that it seemed less rehearsed and more authentic. I was hoping to think outside the box, given my unique vantage point as an immigrant and survivor of addiction. I did not want to be static or fixed in my approach, since my life had certainly not been that way! Ultimately, this mindset allowed me to approach a nerve-wracking period of training with courage and conviction. I was leading a life of self-creation in alignment with my creative soul to serve others.

Fully Exploring Your Story

During my supervised field experience at a Minneapolis organization called Change Inc., Dr. James Nelson, LMFT, led my group. Dr. Nelson encouraged us to share our personal life stories during our sessions. When it was my turn, I found it challenging to express my narrative. This made me realize I had yet to explore and embrace my life experiences fully, which, in turn, sparked my journey of self-discovery. In this moment, I began to understand the significance of reflecting on my experiences to gain self-awareness and comprehend how my past influences my present.

Dr. Nelson emphasized the healing power of stories, which deeply resonated with me. This message inspired me to approach therapy with a deeper appreciation for the power of personal narratives. I now understand that our past experiences shape our perceptions of ourselves, guiding our actions and aspirations for the future.

Remember this: fully exploring our stories leads to awareness, which enables us to understand and discover ourselves more deeply. As we become more aware, we gain the wisdom to create the lives we want. Understanding how past experiences have shaped our present helps us determine how we want to shape our futures. Reflecting on our past and present experiences through self-reflection, journaling, and conversations with family or close friends allows us to better understand what has happened to us. With a deeper understanding of our past experiences and increased awareness of our present lifestyles (and life choices), we can shift our mental perspectives, shaping the lives we dream of creating. The journey towards awareness begins with change, while reconnection with past experiences provides the necessary knowledge to start changing our present and defining our future through confident thinking and behavior.

This deep awareness is intrinsically linked to the creative soul and self-creation. When we understand ourselves and our circumstances more deeply, we free ourselves to think beyond our confines—beyond our present situation—and creatively reflect on how to move forward differently and more productively. Creative thinking challenges us to explore who we are presently and who we want to become. This empowers us to adopt the changes we desire to make in our lives and pushes us to think and behave in ways that best match our most authentic, growing self.

REFLECTION QUESTIONS

Think CREATIVELY about your future. How can you stretch yourself beyond your self-imposed limits? Jot down your thoughts in a notebook if you'd like, and revisit these questions whenever you need.

1. What dreams do you want to materialize?
2. How can you live more authentically in US society?
3. Where are you going in life? Who are you becoming?
4. How do you want to see yourself?
5. What obstacles prevent you from constructing your desired life in this country? How could you start to think and behave differently to work on overcoming?
6. Do you believe in your ability to create a life that feels authentic in the community?
7. What relationship do you dream of building with yourself moving forward? (How will you strengthen your self-nurturing, caring, and loving behaviors in life?)
8. How do you want to engage with and relate to people from various backgrounds?
9. Name one unhealthy thought you frequently have. (For example, you may think you are an unworthy or bad person, rather than believing you are a good person who has experienced bad or unfavorable situations in life.)
10. Name one healthy thought or way to reshape the unhealthy thought pattern identified in the prior question.
11. What dreams are you in the process of creating already?

CHAPTER 6

THE COURAGEOUS SELF AND SELF-DEVELOPMENT

The fourth mental foundation is the courageous self, which enables self-development. Self-*creation* is primarily focused on forming or reconnecting with our authentic self-identity; it is internal work. Once we have established this authentic self-identity, we can engage in self-*development*, which revolves around personal and sociocultural growth, a process that is largely external. With courage, we can continually build and develop ourselves, leading us to the healthy, functioning lives we desire and allowing us to live confidently.

Creation is more about reconnecting with our true selves, while development is about consistently advancing the truth we want to create in the world (internal creation/affirmation versus external action). I see it this way: creation comes before development, but development continually refines creation; they work together as a team. Once we start trusting the creative process, we can sharpen our skills through continuous practice, developing and building on life skills, thinking, and behavioral practices that align with the selves and lifestyles we choose to embrace.

Another way to think about these terms is to view self-development as advancing self-creation. Self-creation involves rebuilding one's life through exploration and discovery of our truth, or reconnecting to the true self through intentional self-awareness. After becoming aware of our authentic selves, we hold the power to keep developing—strengthening this new, authentic, growing version of the self by applying new, healthy thinking patterns, behaviors, and actions. These thought patterns and behaviors should align with the life we consciously choose and dream of building. When we stop developing, we stop advancing the creation process of life; we eventually stop our creativity from growing, preventing us from healing from unfavorable or undesired experiences. This is an important concept for immigrants who have experienced cultural rootlessness because it addresses how we deal with change. We must be able to look inward and give grace to our efforts, despite the measuring sticks we often use when dealing with life's disappointments. We have to believe that we are bigger than the results.

While comparison to others can easily get in the way of our joy, comparison to versions of ourselves can be equally devastating. Given that many immigrants to the United States feel the constant pressure of proving our worth, we can often be unnecessarily harsh on ourselves in ways that breed a toxic mindset. This state of mind will ultimately leave us feeling as though we are running on a hamster wheel, never advancing or able to slow down to appreciate just how far we've come.

What Am I Avoiding Facing in Life?

As we move ever forward, it is important to pay attention to our bodies and their messages of avoidance. In college, when I used to drink, I would often make excuses to avoid exercising, telling myself I would only have one drink. However, I knew deep down that I never planned to stop at just one. Once I started, I would find reasons to keep going. As a result, I would wake up with a hangover, get into arguments, and neglect my studies. It took me a while to realize that these were all the wrong choices, and even though I understood the consequences, it did not stop me until I faced a severe near-death experience, resulting from my refusal to exercise resilience and resist addictive behaviors. I was avoiding the root cause of my alcohol dependence—the trauma that was still clinging to me from my childhood in a war-torn nation paired with my inability to feel wholly comfortable with US culture.

Many of the emotional dilemmas that arise from cultural rootlessness for immigrants could be solved with the age-old question, "What unhealed situations am I avoiding facing in life?" By asking this, we can draw on our most innate experiences, traits, and characteristics that make up our courageous self.

As I navigate the often-unsettling reality of becoming a divorced single father, I find myself skillfully avoiding thoughts that threaten to overwhelm me. Each day, the weight of anxiety looms large, affecting my ability to effectively support, nurture, and raise my child in this new and turbulent environment. The landscape of parenthood, once familiar, has transformed into a complex web of challenges, where shifting developmental needs and evolving relational dynamics are constants that I must learn to manage.

The initial shock of separation made me acutely aware of the dual responsibilities I now bear. I'm not just a parent; I'm also trying to juggle my own emotional recovery as a divorced father while ensuring that my child feels secure and wholly loved. This requires immense courage—the kind that compels me to confront both the painful truths of my past and the realities of my present responsibilities as a parent, regardless of how daunting they may seem.

However, I am determined to adopt a strength-based perspective to face these challenges head-on—to tap into that inner well of courage we all possess. To amplify this courage, I have taken a few different approaches: 1) looking for the positive, 2) reframing a difficult situation as a growth opportunity, and 3) calling upon my community for support when needed.

Allow me to elaborate and put these three concepts in the context of my divorce. First, I actively try to remind myself to look for silver linings and focus on the positives in our lives, no matter how small they seem. In this case, it is a good thing that my wife and I recognized fairly early on in our marriage that our relationship was not working out. We severed ties instead of trying to repair a broken and sometimes toxic relationship.

Secondly, I have found a profound potential for growth and healing in this situation, as I learn to redefine myself as an independent person and a single dad. Lastly, I have found courage by tapping into myself, my family, and my community. My support system strengthens me as a father, allowing me to lean on others' wisdom and experience as I strive to nurture my child in these uncertain times.

As I navigate the complex and often daunting journey of raising my child between two different households, I am constantly aware of the difficulties that may arise. My child's need to adapt to differing household rules and traditions, and the differing dynamics between my home and the home of my child's mother, fills me with unease and concern.

Each day tests my emotional strength as I confront the parental challenges that may arise. I take time to reflect on the actions I can take, such as practicing positive self-talk and reframing negative thoughts into self-empowering affirmations. I remind myself to concentrate on what is within my control, particularly the activities I can engage in with my son during our parenting time to support his healthy development.

My unwavering commitment to my child's well-being and safety is always at the forefront of my mind. I also prioritize modeling a calm and positive presence for my son, teaching him through my actions, serving as a role model, and providing verbal support. My goal as a committed parent is to create a nurturing environment, even amid uncertainty. I focus on fostering positive communication, open-mindedness, and honest interactions with my son and his mother. Additionally, I recognize the importance of demonstrating endless patience as he navigates his feelings about our new family structure. Clear, respectful communication with his mother is another pillar of my parenting, since a cooperative relationship is vital for our child's stability and happiness. These are all examples of courageously redefining myself and my role—stepping into a future filled with unknowns and uncertainties. Everyone must deal with difficult situations at times, and how we choose to face them will determine the road ahead.

Courage and Self-Care

It is difficult to act boldly or courageously if you are feeling less than your best. That is why it is important to engage in the other three C's first—being curious about a new way forward, having compassion for yourself, and considering how to move forward creatively. This is all a form of self-love or self-care.

When dealing with my divorce, I intentionally prioritized self-care, understanding that my personal well-being directly affects my ability to parent effectively. This includes engaging in mindfulness practices, seeking therapy when needed, and making time for activities that recharge my spirit. I also make it a point to dedicate time to enjoyable, child-centered activities that foster our bond and offer my son a sense of normalcy and joy in an otherwise challenging situation.

Concentrating on these manageable aspects of parenting, I aim to tackle this daunting journey confidently, reminding myself to take it one thoughtful step at a time (taking things slow and being patient with yourself is another form of self-care!). As I work through the intricacies of co-parenting, each small victory fills me with courage and hope. It builds my confidence that we can nurture our son and ourselves as we navigate this new chapter together.

I often find myself retreating into contemplation about the painful reality of the moments in my son's life that I will miss because of the divorce. The emotional weight of thinking about missing some of his milestones—the excitement of school performances, academic or developmental achievements, and other instances that will shape his young life—can sometimes feel incredibly overwhelming. Each moment carries a deep longing and loss, knowing I won't always be there to cheer him on or celebrate with him.

However, I recognize the importance of finding the courage to focus on the positives amid this struggle. Despite the absences I cannot change, I remind myself that I still have countless opportunities to play an active role in his development. I will make it my mission to be fully present during our shared moments, cherishing every laugh, conversation, and quiet moment together. I will keep striving to create lasting connections by engaging in activities he enjoys, listening to his thoughts, and being there to meet his needs and desires, both big and small. In these precious moments, I see the opportunity to positively influence his growth and well-being, fostering a bond that transcends any challenges we may face.

If you are dealing with a difficult situation, I encourage you to engage in the difficult (and courageous) act of facing it head-on. When you dare to stare down your troubles, you can begin to have an honest conversation with yourself about how to approach them. From there, you can begin to reframe your situation in order to see the positive aspects of it. This can take time, as it is not always easy to recognize the positive in certain situations at first glance. This is deep work, work that involves reflection, candidness, and a willingness to forge a new path.

The Link Between Courage and Communication

As my family navigates the various stages of our development, I find myself reflecting on how to best communicate about our divorce. This is a significant conversation that requires both sensitivity and thoughtfulness. It is essential to help my son understand that families can go through transitions without the parents' love for their child diminishing in any way. Family systems and family love can take on unique and diverse forms. I want to remind him that many families have diverse structures, and nothing is wrong with that. I will courageously and consistently strive to help him understand that the structure of our family does not take away from his parents' love for him.

Choosing courage over fear is essential. In this situation, being courageous has helped me gain the confidence to support my son's journey. Fear often clouds our perception and causes us to focus only on the negative aspects of our situations. This mindset can trap us in a cycle of doubt and helplessness, making it difficult to see a way forward. It can also make us secretive and silent, keeping our troubles and thoughts to ourselves instead of sharing them candidly. Instead, it is important to cultivate a perspective grounded in courage, which helps us communicate openly, recognize the positive elements in our lives, and confidently grow healthier, more fulfilling lives.

Despite challenges (large or small), it is vital to intentionally embody courage through verbal communication, redirecting thoughts from the negative to the positive, and trying to combat any negative feelings that arise with kindness to yourself and others. In my case, I am applying courage daily in my parenting, with the aim of fostering trust and openness, encouraging honest communication, and helping my son feel safe and comfortable enough to share his thoughts and feelings without fear of judgment.

As a child, I carried memories of my early years enduring a civil war in my home country. I struggled with anxieties about adapting to new environments, meeting new people, and facing different situations. I worried about my uncertain future at school and in the community. I found it challenging to embrace a strong connection to my home country, where my memories were marred by violence, poverty, and a lack of necessities. However, I also did not seamlessly fit into my adopted country, where I was embarrassed by my dark skin tone, my Liberian accent, and the cultural differences between myself and my US peers. On top of all that, I felt reluctant to share my vulnerable feelings, even with those who shared my background or identity. Whenever conversations about the war came up at home or in the Liberian community, I would avoid the topic. As a child, I would ask my parents if I could leave, or I would distract myself with phone games or music. I made a promise to myself that I would never go back to Liberia, feeling as if I had narrowly escaped death and hardships. Eventually, I came to realize that my pain and struggles continued to affect me, even in the United States.

Later on, as I approached the end of my time at St. Olaf College, I realized that I had been ignoring unresolved trauma from my past, failing to communicate my struggles with my peers, a trusted mentor or counselor, or even myself. This was affecting me through nightmares, negative thinking, neglecting self-care, low self-esteem, and struggling with addiction. I was also distancing myself from my spiritual beliefs, avoiding church, and feeling disconnected from my almighty Heavenly Father.

Seeking validation and love from others became a struggle, and I found it difficult to define my sense of identity and self-worth. After graduating from college, facing the future and figuring out who I wanted to be was tricky. I wanted a fulfilling life in the United States, but I felt weighed down by my past and uncertain about my future, since I had still failed to open up about these things. This led to strained relationships with family and loved ones—something I avoided dealing with due to feelings of shame and my tendency to compare myself to societal standards. To mask my pain, I turned to overindulging in the form of watching movies, partying with friends, and overworking instead of addressing my deep internal struggles—instead of reconnecting with my true self, communicating my struggles, and working toward the authentic life I desired.

As I proceeded in my life journey, I began to approach life with greater honesty, authenticity, and communication. My candid evaluations helped me in my efforts, my choices, and my desires. Today, I constantly check in with myself to ask if I am exhibiting behaviors that align with the life I want. This is not always easy to do, since we are all works in progress. However, it is possible to embrace self-improvement with enthusiasm, knowing that it is ultimately medicine for continuing to heal.

Making Courageous Decisions

When I am feeling as though I am too judgmental of myself, I turn to my faith in my Creator's words to find solace in who I am and will continue to be, despite my shortcomings. After many years of wrestling with this process, I have learned that my dreams are not destinations—they are everyday decisions. This shift in mindset takes me out of the hamster wheel and moves me into a place of fullness.

Another major part of making everyday decisions involves being open to changing your mind. I have had to exercise this in many facets of my life. While living in Minnesota, I was dealing with familial stress, fatherhood, and divorce. I felt as though I was struggling to find support and peace in a place I once called home. My joy and true happiness felt absent, I felt out of control, and I was experiencing a period of darkness.

Much of this was because I had made a series of decisions that I thought were aligned with what I wanted, like marrying young. However, I realized that I was romanticizing reality instead of finding true alignment with my dreams. It takes courage to face reality, especially when we've romanticized or distracted ourselves from it. Once I allowed myself to acknowledge that the marriage wasn't working, my heart was broken. After everything I had endured, how could I *not* be on a linear path of progress in life? How could I feel like I was back to square one?

These were the questions I pondered as I worked through my complex feelings. My growing relationship with my God helped me realize that much of my failed marriage had been due to familial pressures. I had allowed others to determine a timeline for me that was not aligned with my own principles of self-mastery. I had not had the courage to make my own decisions that were aligned with my true self.

Once I realized this, I chose self-forgiveness, compassion, and the willingness to be curious and courageous about creating a new authentic life for myself, instead of continually being controlled by damaging thoughts, emotions, and behaviors. Instead of forcing a relationship to achieve the ideal of a successful marriage, I decided to love myself and acknowledge that my marriage wasn't the right fit for either of us, recognizing that this would be a radical and courageous step in my healing journey.

Keep in mind, when faced with complex situations, a "right" decision may not exist. Instead, focus on making the best decision with the information you have while remaining open to adjusting your path if necessary. It is possible to foster self-compassion and acceptance when you accept that some outcomes are beyond your control and you're doing your best to navigate them.

It isn't easy to make a large, life-altering decision like pursuing a divorce, and it is natural to fear the cascade of other changes that can potentially arise. In making the right decision for my life, I had to change where I lived, how I worked, and how I parented. In my clients, I've noticed that it's during these seasons of upheaval when people are most likely to re-experience difficult emotions that remind them of their trauma. It takes courage to walk into the unknown, especially when your memories linked to change or transition include war, relocation, and intense struggle. Any change can seem as dangerous as the high-stakes situations you already encountered, whether or not they actually are.

Courageously facing reality can be heartbreaking. It often comes with acknowledging that our lives are taking different paths than we had planned or hoped. That's why many people turn to alcohol, drugs, overworking, unhealthy relationships or excessive media use to distract or numb themselves and avoid their situations. Courageously facing reality and making major life decisions is difficult, but it can also be liberating. It reveals how some of our anxieties about the future (like the fear of never finding another partner or the fear of letting other people down) are misguided or even untrue. When we start to live in reality and dare to make tough decisions, rather than running away or distracting ourselves, we can begin to shape life in the way we want.

Practices to Build Courage

Since I am committed to following a positive path each day, I have outlined specific strategies for handling difficult situations. My main goal is to use daily reflection to consistently evaluate how my past experiences influence my current thoughts and behaviors. I achieve this through journaling, guided spiritual meditation, prayer, and honestly processing my memories and present life experiences. I also question how I want these experiences to impact my life. These methods are effective for many people, and I encourage you to try them if you haven't already. At first, daily reflection, meditation, or journaling may not feel natural or easy, but the more you practice these affirming acts, the more natural they will feel.

In addition to these courage-building habits, I care for myself physically by maintaining good hygiene, quality sleep, healthy eating habits, and regular exercise. I also engage in activities that bring me joy, alone and with others in my expanding community. I practice honest, positive, and motivating self-talk and consciously steer my thoughts toward positivity and realism, rather than getting caught up in anxious thinking. I remind myself that I can choose how to think and behave genuinely. In any given situation, I might pause to ask myself how I want to interpret my experiences at that moment.

Adopting a positive perspective about ourselves is essential for an effective healing journey. We are not traveling on a path to become some very specific or perfect version of a person we've once imagined. Instead, we are traveling to become someone who is oriented toward progress and self-development. The "self" part of self-development is important to note, given that it is often overlooked through the unhealthy practices of comparison that exist within today's society.

It is also important to keep community and spirituality at the forefront of your mind as you begin to heal. In my case, I proactively seek help and support when necessary, whether through asking for resources, reaching out to loved ones, or sharing stories or experiences with others. My spirituality significantly reduces stress through prayer, meditation, involvement in my spiritual community, and volunteering. It helps me find joy and compassion beyond my daily stresses, and it balances my work, family, relationships, and overall well-being.

In addition to spiritual practices of attending church services, I consistently read the Holy Bible, other books focused on stress management, spiritual growth, healing from trauma, and listening to motivational speeches that support improving one's quality of life. I also like to try new things, such as new methods I've learned in self-improvement books, new recipes, or new activities. Staying curious (the first "C") can help keep your mind nimble and help you move courageously forward.

Another key aspect of the healing journey is practicing positive self-talk and self-affirmation. This involves acknowledging your inner and outer beauty and approaching each day with kindness, compassion, and gratitude. Making an intentional effort to shift your focus from self-criticism to self-appreciation can genuinely transform your mindset. For me, when faced with uncertainty, I prioritize gratitude and reflect on the people and things I am thankful for. I have also realized the importance of managing my emotions and making decisions from a place of calm and balance rather than impulsiveness. I must allow myself to process my emotions before making important decisions.

With intentional effort and daily practices, it is possible to consciously reshape your thought patterns, leading to healthier behaviors and interactions. By prioritizing self-care and embracing imperfections, you can nurture organic and gradual personal growth, foster genuine connections, and effect lasting, positive change. I have found it helpful to set short-term, achievable goals using motivation-driven strategies in all areas of my life, including my career, relationships, and physical health.

Additionally, it is important to live authentically and be discerning about sharing personal information based on the quality of your relationships and understanding the potential consequences of sharing with individuals who may not be trustworthy. Aim to engage in all interactions with intention, authenticity, and mindfulness, recognizing that different relationships call for different levels of closeness and sharing.

Immigrants often have a complex response to change, which is influenced by factors such as their trauma history, support network, and readiness to embrace a new way of life. Their immigration status, including how they arrived in the United States, also plays a significant role. Immigrants arrive in various ways, such as marriage to a US citizen, family sponsorship, educational opportunities, or refugee support organizations. This diversity should remind us to be inclusive and open-minded in supporting immigrants' healing (your own included), no matter their personal path or circumstances. It is essential to remember that immigrants may not trust new experiences outside their cultural norms and may fear losing their core identity to fit into Western society. Taking all these factors into consideration is crucial for supporting and guiding immigrants as they bravely navigate their new lives.

Now, I walk bravely and courageously, knowing that I also have the power to change my mind. My story does not have to look or sound one single way—it is not a movie plot with a perfect ending—and I do not have to exist against the measuring stick of others or my harsher self. I can choose to develop myself with completely different terms and expectations. You, too, can adapt a courageous mindset, built on intentional everyday practices, authentic development, openness, your spiritual higher power, compassion, and love.

REFLECTION ACTIVITY

Move forward with COURAGE. Look over your answers to the other reflection questions from the prior three chapters. Ponder them and consider how you can courageously and fully embrace your past, present, and future selves. How can you move forward with authenticity, while still acknowledging and honoring your roots?

Write out some ideas on how you will boldly carve a new path forward. Be as specific as possible.

CONCLUSION

I want to thank all my readers for staying until the end of this book. Your willingness to engage with me throughout the reading and reflection journey positively displays your resilience and willingness to work on overcoming your suffering. I hope that every moment of shared insight has enriched your experience and contributed to your personal growth. I truly appreciate your commitment to fully engage with the Four Central Healing Foundations tools in this book during this transformative time in your life.

It is important to recognize that cultural traumas can have profound, lasting effects on an individual's overall well-being that can leave them feeling rootless or caught between realities. The interplay between mental and physical health underscores the importance of addressing and healing from trauma, as unresolved issues can create a cycle that perpetuates suffering across various aspects of life.

Effectively addressing trauma requires a comprehensive approach that harnesses both internal psychological resources and external support systems. This dual approach is crucial because one approach or the other may not be wholly effective, but together they can help us heal. Regarding internal resources and practices, an individual may choose to utilize techniques such as mindfulness, self-compassion, journaling, affirmations, or cognitive reframing. These tools can empower individuals to better process their experiences and emotions. Through active reflection and processing, a traumatized individual can move toward healthy growth and overcome various challenges in life. In contrast, external support mechanisms—therapy, support groups, community resources, healthy relationships, cultural centers, and more—provide relational support and professional guidance, which are invaluable during recovery. It is exceedingly difficult to achieve healing on your own, and a trusted collection of external resources and positive relationships can provide much-needed support for longer lasting success.

Gathering authentic resources can help mitigate pain and stressors amid life's challenges. When you're considering external resources and support, remember to be mindful of the influences you allow into your life—whether relational, spiritual, or societal—and critically evaluate how others' values align with your own.

Understanding the significance of our roots is vital, as they form the bedrock of our identity and embody the legacies we inherit. Roots are not merely historical references; they encompass our cultural, spiritual, psychological, social, familial, and personal narratives, influencing the ways we perceive the world and interact with others. When we discuss rootlessness, we often refer to a profound sense of disconnection that can arise from a history marred by traumatic events. Addressing and healing from these past experiences requires consciously exploring cultural history as well as our personal *and* vicarious trauma, and considering how to move forward with these elements in mind (clinging to some of our cultural roots while rejecting the parts that do not serve us). By examining the intricate layers of our experiences—acknowledging both the pain and the resilience that define them—we begin to unravel the complexities that shape us. This mind-and-body healing journey helps us to continually foster a deeper understanding of ourselves through reflection and action-driven steps toward positive changes. Focus on paving the way for authentic healing resources and support networks to flow into your newly defined, constantly growing healthy self.

It's crucial to acknowledge that when we encounter the profound impact of trauma, it can trap us in a seemingly unending cycle of suffering and despair. This cycle is not simply a fleeting phase; it is a deeply rooted pattern that can permeate every facet of our lives, casting a long shadow over our daily experiences. The effects of cultural rootlessness trauma manifest in various ways, including but not limited to a barrage of relentless negative thoughts that cloud judgment and hinder our abilities to see the world. These thoughts are often accompanied by pervasive and frequently distorted beliefs about ourselves, leading us to view ourselves through a lens of inadequacy, shame, or hopelessness. Such self-perceptions can result in self-defeating behaviors that not only perpetuate our pain but also create barriers to healing and growth. It is also important to acknowledge that unresolved trauma has a lasting impact on our daily lives. It can keep us in a constant state of unease, leading to ongoing feelings of anxiety, discomfort, and disconnection. This emotional struggle affects both our minds and bodies. When we remain stuck in the hurting or suffering stages, we struggle to tap into the internal and external support networks and resources needed for us to live our best lives in society.

This is where the Four C's come into play. When we start to build (or rebuild) our curious, compassionate, creative, and courageous healing foundations, we engage in healthy thoughts, kindness (to ourselves and others), unbridled joy, and authentic behaviors. This enables us to lead our lives more honestly and with greater confidence.

In my own life, I recently relied on the Four Central Healing Foundations when making a life-altering decision. After my divorce, I found myself floundering. The life I had so carefully built had been uprooted, and I was forced to navigate a new path—divorced, living in Minnesota once again, and seeking a new job. In my hunt for work, I applied for and was offered a position in a well-known health care system as a family therapist. The work would commence in three or four months. I accepted the position, but I began to feel a sense of wrongness about my decision. On paper, the job seemed like a good fit, but I was having misgivings because I had already performed similar work in the past and I did not feel overly enthusiastic about engaging with this type of work again. Enter the Four C's.

I became **curious** about my feelings of unease and started to reflect on them. Was this the best route for me? Would it be better for myself and my well-being to find a new position, and a new type of challenge? Could a different position also be better for others, since I would potentially be more energized and enthusiastic?

I treated myself with **compassion** during this time of contemplation, giving my body the nourishment, rest, and care it needed. I did not force myself into a decision, and I was not critical of my indecisiveness. Instead, I recognized that this important internal work needed to be done, and it was best to be gentle with myself and take all the time I needed.

When considering the way forward, I began to engage in **creative** thinking. What if I dared to do something totally outside the box—something I had never considered before? What if I sought employment outside of the places I knew so well (Iowa and Minnesota)? Amazingly, in this period between jobs, I received an invitation to apply for a job I would have never thought to consider: working as a mental health therapist and counselor for an Indigenous population in rural Alaska. With my creative mind at work, I began to ponder if this could be the right fit for me—if I could really take such a radical turn in my life. I decided I could make it work, but it would involve a good deal of the fourth C: courage.

Mustering up my **courage**, I applied for the position in Alaska. After interviewing, I was told I got the job, and I was expected to start soon. The news was both exciting and terrifying, as it meant carving out a whole new life—an entirely new existence—in a very remote area unlike anything I had known or experienced. However, I hoped to make a positive difference in the lives of the beautiful Indigenous Yup'ik people of Hooper Bay, Alaska. This population has a history of cultural trauma, co-occurring with individual PTSD, major depression, anxiety, addiction, intimate partner violence, and high suicide rates. The people were in desperate need of a mental health professional. I felt called to the work, and I decided I was courageous enough to pursue it.

Today, I've been living in Hooper Bay, Alaska, population of approximately 1,375, for a few months. The area is beautiful and rugged, perched on the edge of western Alaska on the chilly Pacific Ocean. If I want to travel outside the area, I must go by bush plane. The nearest major city of Bethel is 150 miles away, and it is impossible to travel there by car. Though I am still getting used to such a radically different lifestyle and way of being, I am confident I made the right decision. Using the Four C's, I stretched beyond the limits of what I thought was possible to carve out a new life for myself—a life of my choosing that feels right to me.

By dedicating ourselves wholeheartedly to genuine self-exploration, self-discovery, self-creation, and self-development, we empower ourselves to cultivate greater resilience and openness to a new, healthy, and genuine lifestyle, chosen by us with confidence. As we engage in our unique transformative processes, we must create a space for authentic understanding, nurturance, care, and loving behaviors to flourish, enriching our lives and the lives of those around us.

I invite all my readers to review the questions found at the end of each chapter with a fresh mindset and a genuine commitment to honesty. Instead of simply viewing these questions as tasks to be completed, strive to see them as tools for developing a deeper connection with your growing self-identity and the life you dream of building. By thoughtfully engaging with these questions, you can better understand your current situation and evaluate how it aligns with the person you wish to become. It is essential to carefully explore, discover, create, and develop your answers and the action steps that best align with your true purpose and vision of life, moving forward with confidence each day.

To continually work on accomplishing your truth, work on slowly but intentionally embracing your healing journey as a priority in your daily life. As you engage with this work, I encourage you to keep working on establishing and strengthening your four core foundations by building your curious mindset, compassionate heart, creativity, courage, and belief systems. Consider the foundations that best represent your desires for creating a more authentic sense of self and life. You have the power to foster a richer and more fulfilling life and to boldly move forward.

RESOURCES

The Holy Bible (King James Version).

Today's Light Devotional Bible (English Standard Version). St. Louis: Concordia Publishing House, 2014.

Bright, Nancee Oku, director. *Liberia: America's Stepchild.* PBS (United States), 2022. 1 hr., 30 min. https://www.pbs.org/wgbh/globalconnections/liberia/.

Van der Kolk, Bessel. *The Body Keeps the Score: Brain, Mind, and Body in the Healing of Trauma*. New York: Penguin Books, 2015.

Cabacungan, Renne. "Identity Formation and the Immigrant Experience," Duquesne Scholarship Collection. April 20, 2022. https://dsc.duq.edu/urss/2022/proceedings/8.

Morgan-Trostle, Juliana, Kexin Zheng, Carl Lipscombe. "The State of Black Immigrants." Black Alliance for Just Immigration and New York University's Immigrant Rights Clinic, 2016.

American Immigration Council Staff. "Data Snapshot: The Number of Black Immigrants in the US Continues to Rise." *Immigration Impact*. February 9, 2024. https://immigrationimpact.com/2024/02/09/data-number-of-black-immigrants-in-the-us/.

Schumacher, Shannon, Liz Hamel, Samantha Artiga, et al. "Understanding the U.S. Immigrant Experience: The 2023 KFF/LA Times Survey of Immigrants." *KFF.org*. September 17, 2023. https://www.kff.org/report-section/understanding-the-u-s-immigrant-experience-the-2023-kff-la-times-survey-of-immigrants-findings/.

ACKNOWLEDGMENTS

I am thankful for my publisher, Wise Ink Media, and other key members of my publishing team, including creative director and project manager Victoria Petelin. I truly appreciate their support and guidance throughout the creation of this book. I am also grateful for my undergraduate institution, St. Olaf College; my graduate degree program in Argosy University, Twin Cities; and Change Inc., located in Minneapolis, Minnesota.

ABOUT THE AUTHOR

Alfred C. Jaryan Jr., LMFT, is a licensed marriage and family therapist who has dedicated his career to helping individuals overcome trauma and cultural rootlessness. His professional journey, combined with personal experiences, has shaped the content of this book.

Birth Country: Monrovia, Liberia, 1989–1999
Iowa City, IA: 1999–2001
Hometown: Bloomington, MN, 2001–2008
High School: John F. Kennedy High School, Bloomington, MN, 2004–2008
Undergraduate Education: St. Olaf College, Northfield, MN. Bachelor of Social Work degree (BSW), 2008–2012
Graduate School: Argosy University, Twin Cities, Eagan, MN. Master of Marriage & Family Therapy degree, MFT, 2013–2016
Board Experience: Change Inc., board of directors, 2023–2024
Email: alfredjaryan35@yahoo.com

BOOK ALFRED TO SPEAK

Alfred C. Jaryan Jr., LMFT, speaks about overcoming cultural rootlessness traumas and healing in curious (open-minded), compassionate, creative, and courageous ways to live a whole life. Mastering the art of true healing requires a journey of authentic self-exploration, self-discovery, self-creation, and self-development. We can provide the most effective healing for ourselves. Still, we first need awareness of the problem before we can implement any powerful tools. True healing will challenge our beliefs so we can become open to new possibilities. There is a new way forward that our spirit inherently craves, but it requires discipline. True healing involves applying honest cultural, spiritual, mental, and social guidance, which will bring forth your most authentic self to the world more confidently. Finding your whole, authentic self is an essence of healing that respects cultural differences, allowing for our beautiful cultural, spiritual, mental and social aspects of life to burst with vibrancy and positively impact others.

www.ingramcontent.com/pod-product-compliance
Lightning Source LLC
LaVergne TN
LVHW020650100826
845148LV00012B/2406

* 9 7 8 1 6 3 4 8 9 8 4 6 1 *